WE'RE AN EXAMPLE OF
TRAJECTORIES AND VICTORIES
HIP-HOP, EDUCATION AND LITERACIES OF REEXISTENCE

By
Ana Lúcia Silva Souza

Translated By
Ayala Tude, Tanya L. Saunders and Feva Omo
Iyanu

AMÉFRICA
PRESS

ISBN: 979-8-9872776-1-4 (Paperback)
ISBN: 979-8-9872776-3-8 (eBook)

First English Translation Printed Edition 2024

Améfrica Press
P.O. Box 24647
Baltimore, MD 21214 USA www.amefricapress.com

First Published in Portuguese in São Paulo, Brazil in 2020 as: Letramentos De
Reexistência: poesia, grafite, música, dança: hip hop
Publisher: Parábola Editorial Rua Dr. Mário Vicente, 394 - Ipiranga
04270-000 São Paulo, SP www.parabolaeditorial.com.br ISBN 978-85-7934-032-1
This is an authorized translation from the Portuguese language edition published by
Parábola Editorial

CONTENTS

FOREWORD

We're an Example of Trajectories and Victories: Hip-Hop, Education and Literacies of Reexistence
Patricia Hill Collins December 2023

It is an honor for me to write the Foreword of *We're an Example of Trajectories and Victories: Hip-Hop, Education and Literacies of Reexistence*, the English translation of *Letramentos de Reexistencia: poesia, grafite, musica, dança: hip hop,* by Dra. Ana Lúcia Silva Souza. This important study examines how young people, who are hip-hop's creators and practitioners, engage hip-hop as a form of critical literacy. Now that I have the English translation in front of me, it's ironic that I could not read this book when I initially encountered it. I first met Ana Lúcia Silva Souza at a Critical Applied Linguistics Conference in Brazil and was immediately intrigued by her project. Ever generous, she gave me a copy of her book in Portuguese and did her best to share the broad brushstrokes of her project with me. Yet we were both hampered by the limits of not being able to speak each other's language. Communicating with the help of translators helped, but it was not enough. That exchange left me saddened by the reality of not being able to read her book in Portuguese. I have been waiting for this translation of *Letramentos* into English as part of a broader need for tools to help people who share common concerns bridge the cultural and linguistic barriers that separate us. In this case, *We're an Example of Trajectories and Victories* offers a glimpse into the significance of hip-hop for the world-building projects of a small group of young people in São Paulo. This book has important things to say about how people on the bottom not only criticize oppression but create new forms of humanity for *themselves while doing so.*

As agents of knowledge, the young people in *We're an Example of Trajectories and Victories* know that they are oppressed within intersecting systems of power. They see how being young, poor and black within Brazil denies them opportunities and limits their horizons. But rather than trying to fit in by accepting the status quo or waiting for adults to save them, the youth in this study use hip-hop to develop critical literacy about their situation. Using hip-hop as a site of cultural creation for world-building projects in their everyday lives enables them to criticize the social conditions around them. It helps them to imagine new possibilities for themselves within and beyond everyday life. In this regard, this study stands out from common approaches to hip-hop that focus on the content of its lyrics, or offer ethnographies of hip-hop communities, or that, more recently, celebrate the milestone of hip-hop's 50-year history. Through this careful treatment of youth as creators and practitioners of hip-hop, *We're an Example of Trajectories and Victories* invokes broader theoretical and political questions concerning resistant knowledge from below.

We're an Example of Trajectories and Victories offers a feel for why hip-hop takes the forms that it does among young people who face a common existential question that confronts each generation – what is my place and purpose in the world? Through meticulous fieldwork, this book invites us into the social world of a small group of young people in the periphery of São Paulo, Brazil, who are grappling with this question. We are invited into an up close and personal space that shows how critical literacy happens. As an active participant in her study, Ana Lúcia Silva Souza explores how young people create knowledge, not just by examining the products of their work once it reaches the general public, but rather by spending time with young people to participate in the processes of creating hip-hop. Refusing to treat young people as objects of knowledge, *We're an Example of Trajectories and Victories* looks at hip-hop from the inside out. It centers young people as agents of knowledge that aim to reflect their worldviews. Through their art, their music and the new relationships that they craft with one another, the young people in this study criticize the terms of their current existence as part of reimagining existence beyond places of subordination. They know that São Paulo and Brazil offer them limited opportunities and resist making a place for them in society. In response, young people have claimed the power of creativity to criticize the societies in which they live, and to engage in the critical task of imaging new possibilities for themselves.

Because hip-hop is simultaneously, and intensely, local and increasingly global, the young people whose voices we hear in *We're an Example of Trajectories and Victories* are not alone. Their project is a part of an ever-expanding corpus of work on resistant knowledge from below, one that reflects the voice and aspirations of people who are subordinated within intersecting systems of power. Increasingly, studies of hip-hop view hip-hop as an art form that cultivates a generational discourse among young people who, like the youth in *We're an Example of Trajectories and Victories*, embrace cultural politics as their site of political engagement. A project grounded in creativity—of music, dance, rapping, deejaying, fashion, graffiti and style—the cultural politics of hip-hop offers an array of strategies that links a generation growing up in the ghettos of U.S. inner-city New York, banlieues of the suburbs of Paris as well as the neighborhoods of the *periferia* in São Paulo. The existence of hip-hop writ large is evidence of the power of resistant knowledge. But the complexity of hip-hop raises new questions. There is no one signature form of hip-hop, but rather multiple local hip-hop projects where youth call out the social problems that they face, where creativity and art are shields against oppression.

We're an Example of Trajectories and Victories also signals the growing respect afforded to many projects of resistant knowledge that, while important to their creators, remain unknown, forgotten or suppressed. In this regard, the young people in *We're an Example of Trajectories and Victories* are a part of a broader global movement where people who face varying forms of political domination claim the power of the word to speak for themselves and create new realities. Despite the promise of this view from below, such projects face some fundamental headwinds. Each resistant knowledge project produced within a particular linguistic context, in this case Brazilian Portuguese, finds itself limited to the linguistic worldview of that tradition. Moreover, multiple colonial traditions leave us with a legion of intellectual gatekeepers whose translations of resistant knowledge like hip-hop can change the spirit of the initial project. Multiple expressions of hip-hop exist, but how do we understand the varying forms that hip-hop has taken across place and time, and among varying people, without translations that respect the cultural politics of the product?

I am more convinced of the need for translations such as this one as essential tools for broader struggles for social justice. But the issues of translation are far broader than my initial frustration with being unable to read or speak Portuguese. I read *We're an Example of Trajectories and Victories* as itself an exemplar of the importance of translation, just as Ana Lúcia took seriously her role as a translator of the richness and vibrancy of two interpretive communities, namely the commitment to critical literacy within academic venues, such as the conference where we met, and the care she took during fieldwork in talking with young people, and in trying to understand their point of view. Her intellectual rigor enabled her to write a stellar book that is itself a translation for those of us who can neither become experts in critical literacy nor travel to São Paulo and spend time with young people. *We're an Example of Trajectories and Victories* is a careful and respectful translation of what she found. In this regard, we are fortunate to receive a translation of her intellectual work, one that demonstrates the power of critical literacy for advancing the common concern of social justice.

Editor's Note: Please note, that in the publishing of this book, forced justification was used to make the text fit the page. As a result, the reader may notice some minor formatting errata in this text. The errata do not affect the flow of the book nor the quality of this marvelous translation. However, we are aware of the issue and will address it in the next printing.

PREFACE

The book *We're an Example of Trajectories and Victories: Hip-Hop, Education and Literacies of Reexistence* inaugurated a new phase in Brazilian hip-hop studies when originally released in 2011.

Hip-hop Studies in Brazil began in the 1990s, with Elaine Nunes de Andrade's master's thesis entitled *Black Youth Movement: A Case Study on Young Rappers from São Bernardo do Campo* (1996). Since then, scholars have focused on tracing the origins of this movement in the country, and its connection to the Black diaspora, by demonstrating hip-hop's role in the education and identity formation of the country's Black youth and youth from the periphery.[1] These first steps were fundamental in challenging what were traditionally seen as "objects" of importance for academic research. Those steps also opened doors for research that considers the potential of young Black and peripheral people as social and political protagonists. Unfortunately, these youth did not receive the recognition they deserved in different areas of knowledge production.

In this work, Dra. Ana Lúcia Silva Souza shifts and expands the focus of Brazilian academic production dedicated to hip-hop. If, until

1   Translators' Note (T.N.): *Periferia* or "periphery" are the outskirts of a city. In the Brazilian context, the term refers to working-class suburbs. Generally, those who live in the *periferia* are low-income or poor people. In the writing of this translation, the *periferia* is reimagined as a site of civic engagement, no longer based solely on violence and misery. We have chosen to use the term in Portuguese, rather than in English because it gives a better idea of the meanings it conveys. Editor's Note (E.N.): The United States' concept of "the hood," or the term "the ghetto," is a term that closely reflects the idea, epistemology and experience of the *periferia* in Brazil. The goal here is to convey convergences in the *feelings, lived experiences* and the *power relations* shaping these spaces in the U.S. and Brazil, especially as there are convergences in their emergence, structure and policing. The demography of both spaces is rooted in a history of Black migrant populations from geographical locations understood to be Black spaces/regions. In this case the geographical areas are the Brazilian Northeast and the U.S. Southeast (which are both a part of what scholars refer to as the "Black Atlantic"). Black folks and non-white Afro descendants migrated from these spaces to urban centers from regions of both countries that are racialized and stigmatized as poverty stricken and backwards. We are not translating *periferia* as "the hood" or the "ghetto" because there are contextual, historical and cultural differences that preclude their interchangeability.

its publication, studies on this socio-cultural phenomenon were objects of study for those dedicated to thinking about youth, the periphery and Black identity, the author's book now gains centrality in the area of her intellectual production: applied linguistics. This means that while this book is important for those interested in Black youth cultural manifestations such as hip-hop, it is also important for broader areas of knowledge that gain much from studying this movement. In this case, this book is yet another opportunity to broaden the scope and vision of applied linguistics. Thus, her book has become an oft-referenced work in the area of language studies, and it is almost mandatory reading for understanding literacies based on non-hegemonic experiences and historically minoritized groups.

The discussion presented here allows us to navigate the history of education in Brazil, telling and retelling its chapters based on Black experiences of exclusion and *reexistence*. The latter concept refers to pursuing alternatives in education and Black empowerment that confront an almost predestined path created by racism, one that leads us to examples of trajectories and victories. To do this, the conversation establishes a connection between different historical periods, from slavery to contemporary movements—especially hip-hop—demonstrating how the educational agenda has always been a priority for this ethnic-racial group. Their learning does not exclusively happen in the classroom but is mobilized by socio-cultural movements such as literature, alternative press and music, for example. All of this is connected in the disciplinary framework of language studies, Black studies and the production of Black intellectuals.

To measure the impact of young *rappers* as agents of literacy, the book meticulously portrays the social, political and economic context in which *reexistence* literacies are produced, by highlighting the educational indicators on access to education, permanence in school and learning through an intersectional analysis of race/color, class and generation. The author demonstrates how inequalities in access latently affect Black people who, throughout history, have had to create alternatives to counter statistics and insert themselves into the literate universe in their own ways.

Culture is presented here as an instrument of political agency and discipline. Cultural expressions enable the organization of a narrative and a repertoire for the affirmation of groups whose histories, aesthetics and contributions are denied by Brazilian society, all elements resulting from colonialism, slavery and racism. There is one cultural expression that the author highlights to exemplify these forms of self-affirmation—the hip-hop movement. To this end, drawing from Stuart Hall and Bakhtin as analytical references to support her argument, the author presents identity as a discursive element in, and driver of, transformative collective agencies.

In this book, hip-hop is properly situated as a cultural production of the Black diaspora. It is situated in the Brazilian context, where the author's research experience takes place, and is carried out in partnership with young *rappers* from the city of São Paulo. The transformations of this urban landscape, filled with great social contradictions, are presented to frame the complex environment in which the participants of this research are embedded. The work gives space to the voice and protagonism of these young people as hip-hop educators, moving them from the position of research objects to that of subjects with agency. As the author demonstrates, this relationship between the movement and education leads to institutionality—the occupation of spaces in civil society organizations and the state. Its potential for transformation and mobilization draws the attention of institutions that need to establish constant dialogue with society, especially in systematically marginalized areas.

The spaces of literacy practices where the author develops her argument are spaces where the organization and collective interventions of young *rappers* occur and are where young *rappers* experience taking possession of knowledge. Hip-hop languages are configured as ways that youth construct possibilities for learning and to place themselves into the literate world. In this way, the author makes it clear how literacy does not only happen in the classroom and in school but can also manifest itself in the actions of groups that have been historically excluded and expelled from the school environment.

Hip-hop in Brazil, especially rap, has produced a variety of work that records social dynamics and offers a broad repertoire for understanding Brazilian realities such as the formation of peripheries, inequalities, racial relations, Black music, anti-racist struggles, public security policies, masculinity, social relations, gender, survival alternatives and expectations of the country's poorest population. Due to the significance of these works, the productions of different rap groups have gained space in school and non-school education, as well as in academic research that seeks to record the historical, social, cultural, identitarian and political aspects of society. Rap lyrics, as everyday narratives, highlight the realities the population faces and how different groups—considering race, gender and class—relate and reproduce inequalities and differences.

Interviews, workshops and *rodas de conversa* (conversation circles) were held with a group of young *rappers* from São Paulo. The discussions served as a reference not only for the author's work, but for the organization of these young people's own path as educators. In this way, it was not just the narratives of hip-hop educators that were analyzed. The researcher's way of producing narratives was also analyzed. This is important because the researcher's narrative influences the way the researcher organizes the hip-hop educators' narratives and impacts the recognition of the educators' work.

In this research, Souza demonstrates how work on hip-hop pedagogy opens a space for educators of all kinds. When they are given the freedom to put that pedagogy into practice it contributes to its legitimacy. This means, in other words, that it is necessary to recognize that those named as "educated," and those named as "students," have strategies and practices that contribute to training, so everyone has an important role in educational development.

This study, which presents hip-hop as an educational movement, strengthens the production of tools that will be used for the implementation of the Law 10.639/03 and its *Guidelines for Ethnic-racial Relations Education* and for the *Teaching of Afro-Brazilian and African History and Culture*, which is required by Brazilian law. The hip-hop generation has gone beyond the limits placed by an exclusionary society and created alternatives for the production and creation of knowledge, and alternative learning methodologies. We can see that it has contributed to different areas of training, such as history, geography, physics, chemistry, literacy, mathematics, sociology and the arts. This is because practicing the elements of hip-hop culture requires calculation, skill, sense of confidence, reflection, critical thinking skills, textual analysis, reading and improvisational techniques. A DJ cannot perform without mathematical concepts, a breakdancer cannot train without mastering both the performance space and their body, an MC cannot write a song without language skills and textual analysis, a graffiti artist cannot produce their work without understanding how to conceive and execute a project, without knowing the symmetry of the lines, without alchemizing the chemistry of colors.

Rappers are, in this study, emerging agents with important knowledge in the field of education, which, even today, has difficulties dealing with youth cultures as mobilizers, educators and transformers. Their voices give dimension to the vision they have about education and their roles as educators, which are still seldom recognized in formal educational environments. Sociability, interaction and social identities are elements this study values as markers for understanding the particularities of hip-hop as a Black educational movement. Here the experience of reading, and the universe of language in the lives of young people, is analyzed based on their own elucidations and meanings.

From all this experience, the author develops her innovative concept of *reexistence* in the fields of language studies, cultural studies and the social sciences. This idea helps us understand the cultural spaces present in the *periferias* of the entire country, those that are extremely important for producing meaning and feelings of belonging, spaces where the population builds, and enjoys speaking and listening, while creating the collectivity necessary for its *reexistence*— which is fundamental for the daily survival of these territories and populations. *Reexisting* means reinventing, reformulating, redeeming, celebrating and practicing despite the exclusionary models that shape our society.

Dr. Jaqueline Lima Santos
Assistant Professor of Anthropology
UNICAMP, Campinas, Brazil
2011-2012 Hip-Hop Archive Fellow
The Hutchins Center for African and African American Research
Harvard University

TRANSLATION NOTE

Translating a book is not an easy task. Choosing words that effectively communicate something from one language into a different language is quite a challenge. The way we combine words to create sentences that convey an idea can set in motion a diversity of images, worlds, concepts and perspectives. Translation is a great exercise in decoding thoughts in distinct languages, but it can also be a catastrophic exercise if we ignore what is expressed in the words that are not spoken aloud.

During the translation of *We're an Example of Trajectories and Victories: Hip-Hop, Education and Literacies of Reexistence*, it felt like we were establishing a constant conversation with Dra. Ana Lúcia Silva Souza. It felt as if we were taking part in the conversations she held, like we were having a direct dialogue with the young people she interviewed to develop her research. The conversation started the moment we began thinking about how we would translate the title of the book in a way that reflects the critical and methodological approaches developed by the author.

After long conversations and thoughts on the possible names we could give to the English version of this book, we considered the lyrics of one of the most well-known raps by Racionais MCs, one of the most famous Brazilian hip-hop groups. The title is based on "Negro Drama," a track from their album *Sobrevivendo no Inferno* [Surviving in Hell] (1997), a powerful commentary on the social and racial inequalities prevalent in Brazilian society. Racionais MCs use rap music both as a medium and a pedagogical tool to voice the experiences and perspectives of those often marginalized and oppressed. The literacies of *reexistence* are embedded both in the ideas shared among the young research participants and in the lyrics "Sou exemplo de vitórias, trajetos e glórias," ("I'm an example of victories, trajectories and glories"). Thus, a play on the lyrics "we're an example of victories, trajectories [and glories]" felt like a suitable title of the English version of this book. Conceptualizing rap and hip-hop as tools to educate young people are approaches that Professor Ana Lúcia Silva de Souza also uses to develop her research. Hip-hop, in this sense, is not only related to its elements, but understood as an instructional method that has diverse aesthetic features to promote education from a non-hegemonic perspective.

While reading the book, you may notice that some other terms, such as *"rodas de conversa,"* were left in Portuguese because, besides naming the research methodology developed by the author, we understand that some concepts are specific to describing a cultural approach unique to Brazilian research. In this sense, the conversations among the research participants attempt to maintain the informal aspects of the "Black Portuguese" or "Pretoguês," a term Black Brazilian feminist and intellectual Lélia Gonzalez coined. We also left a lot of the stylistic conventions of the original in this translation. How we address the translation of stylistic approaches to writing is something we are still debating as we develop as a press.

Some slang words from the Portuguese language are thus explained in the footnotes or left in Portuguese, when the English language does not fully express the idea we wanted to convey. That is the same reason why we chose to keep the word *"periferia"* in Portuguese, even though it can be translated to English as "hood" or "periphery." Although there is an equivalent word, the idea it conveys is not the same because, for us, being from the *periferia* encompasses a realm of different perspectives and subjectivities that embody a whole different social experience for the individuals who are born and raised in places located at the physical and social margins of the cities.

We hope that you learn as much as we learned during the process of translating this book, and that these pages resonate across linguistic and cultural landscapes and transport you to new realms. In this shared exploration of words and worlds, we wish you moments of joy, reflection and discovery.

- Ayala Tude, December 1, 2023, Salvador, Bahia, Brazil

STARTING THE CONVERSATION

Hip-hop — far beyond the expression in English that one can literally translate as rocking [*to hip*] the hip [*hop*] — has been understood as an urban youth social movement, rooted in the segment of the population with low purchasing power, the majority of whom are Black[2] and young. *Hip-hop* historically gained strength in the United States from the late 1970s on and later spread to the world's major metropolises.

The *hip-hop* universe is marked by the reflection and criticism it makes concerning social and racial inequalities through poetry, gestures, speech, readings, writings and the images that take shape through the expressiveness of the four artistic elements, namely: the master of ceremonies — MC, the disc jockey — DJ, the dancer — *b-boy* or *b-girl*, and the graffiti artist.

The dynamic *performance* of the dancers, the graffiti artists' drawings, the poetry recited by the MCs and the manipulation of electronic equipment performed by a DJ — the articulation of these four artistic elements constitutes the base of *hip-hop* culture's repertoire (Andrade 1996; Silva 1999).

The most expressive face of *hip-hop* is anchored in *rap* — the sung poetry that, to exist, requires the combination of two elements: the DJ and the MC. The MC is the poet who writes and sings the rap lyrics; the DJ sets the tone for the speech, which generally tackles issues related to social inequalities, racism, discrimination and violence of all kinds.

---

2   E.N.: Black is capitalized throughout the text in order to highlight how Blackness is not just about people who identify with a racial category, but how it also refers to the political dimension of Blackness as an anti-racist subjectivity and culture, especially in a Brazilian context where dis-identification with Blackness is encouraged.

Since *hip-hop* arrived in Brazil in the late 1980s, *hip-hop* culture has become increasingly complex. It brings together various currents or trends for making sense of, seeing and acting on reality. One of these currents focuses on activities of a contestatory and propositional nature, from a political point of view, that deal with the precarious living conditions of a large part of the population. Above all, this is what it means to be a *rapper*[3] — to disseminate the narratives of everyday life by showing how people live, what their dreams are, their needs are and the ways they individually or collectively face problems.

Hip-hop culture draws attention due to its ability to attract a large number of young people to its proposed activities: festivals, workshops and meetings involving the creation of graffiti, dance and music performances, video production and the circulation of informative materials via print, electronic or digital mediums.

For many activists, *hip-hop* is a space for cultural and political production in which a series of socio-linguistic practices are mobilized and used according to their needs. By utilizing linguistic practices, whether in their oral, written or visual modalities, they engage in literacy practices understood as "a set of social practices that use writing both as a symbolic system and as a technology in specific contexts" (Kleiman 1995, 19).

Such literacy practices are focused on the concreteness of the activists' lives, relating to cultural and political issues, and aiming, somehow, to expand their possibilities of insertion in a position of criticism, contestation and subversion, in which, as subjects of rights and knowledge producers, they can forge spaces and act inside and outside the community in which they live. Being part of these places puts them in a complex network of social relations where, through their speech, the occupation and support of forms of social participation committed to the transformations of social and racial relations are negotiated.

It is precisely the complexity of this process that led me to investigate the literacies in *hip-hop* culture, which necessarily implies

---

3   Within a Brazilian context, *rapper* or *hip-hopper* is the term that designates people who are members of the *hip-hop* universe, through any of its expressions (Lindolfo Filho, 2005; Jovino, 2005).

learning to inquire how its insertion instigates unique practices of reading, writing and orality as well as how it affects the construction of the social identities of those involved.

We're an Example of Trajectories and Victories: Hip-Hop, Education and Literacies of Reexistence has, as an analytical *corpus*, a set of data generated through surveys, collective interviews — the *rodas de conversa*,[43] individual interviews and autobiographical writings, in addition to the audiovisual record of a lecture and the cover of a CD produced by a group of activists of the *hip-hop* cultural movement from the *periferia* of São Paulo. The objects of analysis were, mainly, the statements of the participants of the group obtained from oral/verbal interaction, seeking to understand, both linguistically and discursively, the effects of one's insertion in *hip-hop's* community participation: the processes of literacies of the group, and how their social identities are configured and permeated by their cultural movement.

---

4   E.N.: For this book, we use the Brazilian term *rodas de conversa*. *Rodas de conversa* is a popular methodological tool in Brazilian activist circles and in socially engaged research, primarily within the area of education studies. Adamy EK et al (2018) published an English language article where *rodas de conversa* is translated as "conversation circles." Though this translation makes sense, it does not convey the methodological specificity of the concept, nor highlight Brazilian scholars and activists' contributions to academic research methodologies. In the *rodas de conversa*, the researcher becomes a part of the social context in which they are researching in the sense that, even if they are not a part of that community, they are still embedded within the social context by their presence and must negotiate their presence in various moments. The *rodas de conversa* flattens the researcher's relationship with those whose lives they seek to understand by creating a space of open dialogue. Moura & Lima (2014) write the following in their Portuguese language article entitled, A Reinvenção da Roda: Roda de Conversa: Um Instrumento Metodológico Possível: When we talk about the *rodas de conversa*, the initial image that comes to us is of the informal, familiar conversations that are being lost in time, such as the dialogues born around the dinner table or the kitchen table, while the grandmother made fried cake for us to eat with a warm coffee, a space to update what had occurred in the family and in the community and to share joys and sorrows, a moment to open the soul and hearts... This is also the case with the rodas de conversa, when used as a research instrument, a conversation in an environment conducive to dialogue, in which everyone can feel comfortable sharing and listening, so that the spoken, the conversational is relevant to the group and even arouses attention in listening. In rodas de conversa, dialogue is a unique moment of sharing, because it presupposes an exercise of listening and speaking, in which several interlocutors are gathered, and the moments of listening are more numerous than those of speech. The placements of each participant are constructed through interaction with the other, either to complement, disagree, or to agree with the immediately preceding speech. (100) — Translated by Tanya L. Saunders

See: Adriana, F. M., & Maria Glória Lima. (2014). A reinvenção da roda: Roda de conversa, um instrumento metodológico possível. Universidade Federal da Paraíba. Revista Temas Em Educação, 23(1), 95-103.

See: Adamy EK, Zocche DAA, Vendruscolo C, Santos JLG, Almeida MA. Validation in grounded theory: rodas de conversa as a methodological strategy. Rev Bras Enferm [Internet]. 2018;71(6):3121-6. DOI: http:// dx.doi.org/10.1590/0034-7167-2017-0488

GOALS

- To identify the aspects that reveal *hip-hop* as an emerging literacy agent in the speech of the activists selected.

- To identify the literacy practices specific to the *hip-hop* cultural universe in the speech of the research participants.

- To discuss, from an enunciative-discursive approach, the ways that individuals perceive themselves as *hip-hop* activists and literate individuals in verbal interactions, and how those perceptions are built into verbal interactions.

- To understand the particularities that inform the development of the social practices used in written and oral language, in non-school social and cultural contexts, and the possible effects of these engagements on the development of subjects as community literacy agents.

GUIDING QUESTIONS

- What social uses of language in *hip-hop* allow us to characterize it as an agent of literacy?

- What are the particularities of the cultural speaking practices present in the speech of the group participating in the research that led them to be named literacy agents?

- Is it possible to speak about literacies of resistance, since the practices and the literacy events of the activists engaged in the *hip-hop* movement come from their contesting identities?

- In their interactions, how do participants convey meanings, produce and communicate their identities as *hip-hop* activists, and how do these proclaimed identities produce movements of identification, differentiation and readjustment in interactions?

From this moment on, answering these questions will be our journey.

CHAPTER 1

THE WAYS OF "DOING": DEVELOPING THIS RESEARCH

(...) when Analu said: I'm doing some stuff like this, like that, did you see that I was the first one to say: is it just one more term paper to be kept over there in the *playboizada* (*rich kids*) schoolbooks? I was the first one to say that, bro, understand? that's when she turned around and said: noooo, I'm doing this, this and this...
(Dimenor)

t is interesting to show how, dialogically, the threads of knowledge and multiple questionings of meaning and contradictions were pulled and shared to give life to the diverse social voices that sustained the verbal interactions of the *rodas de conversa*, interviews and workshops held for the development of this book. Here I share the details that guided the process of approaching the group of participants, as well as the ethical implications, guidelines and commitments that guided the formation of this group. I also present the research instruments, the data-generating situations and the research participants.

Regarding the process of data generation, coherent with the perspective adopted by the thematic project "Teacher Training: Recontextualization Processes and Literacy Practices,"[5] I adopted an ethnographic approach, considering that realities are different and impossible to compare; the researcher has to immerse themselves in realities to get to know them. Interaction is a way to understand the roles and social places one occupies, as well as the values and attitudes involved in the situations forged in and through the research. In terms of analysis, I also opted for a qualitative approach, favoring an interpretive focus on statements to capture the meanings, values and affects attributed to literacy practices in *hip-hop* and their impact on the participants' process of building their identities.

DATA GENERATION PROCESS

Speech is not ready-made; it is built in the interactions between researchers and the objects of research. This does not always happen like a magic trick, as some sectors of academia sometimes believe. As Lahire (2002, 31) notes, "Words do not wait for a sociologist to come and collect them." The situations I experienced from the beginning to the end of this research broadened my understanding of "being careful about the outlined methodological paths" (Lahire 2002, 31). In the relationship with the subjects who agreed to be co-constructors of this research, I realized that a study that intends to be serious is not only careful; above all, we need commitment.

What is this commitment about? Simply thanking the participants for the testimonies and interviews I received from them? If I ever thought that was enough, the subjects of my research told me loud and clear, "No." The organization and development of this book took on a unique shape and dynamic when the research participants declined the invitation and said, "We no longer want to be treated as research objects for scholars who come here to earn a title." This was the lesson I learned when I made the first and only contact with one of the groups. The "battle" of ideas had already begun. The initial approaches, which seemed frustrating at first, turned out to be fundamental for the work that was later developed with another group.

---

5   Formação do professor: Processos de retextualização e práticas de letramento is a project developed by the research group "Letramento do professor," coordinated by Dr. Angela Kleiman and composed of more than 30 researchers from six different universities in Brazil.

In August 2003, I contacted a group that would not participate in the data generation process that began a year later. What at first seemed like a peaceful approach soon turned into anxiety and discomfort. During our meeting, I told them about my work in the studies of race relations and my activism in the Black movement, which led me to have an affective connection to *hip-hop* and respect for the work of the group, which, among other activities, promoted reading practices in diverse environments. I attributed an important place and value to them for Black youth.

After listening to me carefully, some of the young people in the group started talking about their frustrations with the academic world. They said they had been the subjects of studies on several occasions and yet knew little or nothing about the development and conclusion of the works, except when they saw them published, sometimes without even having a copy for themselves.

They were tired of the situation and no longer wanted to be involved, even though they knew about my history in the Black movement. Nevertheless, they asked me to send the project by e-mail. Faced with a less-than-warm reception, I withdrew. At that moment, I lacked the elements to address the many meanings that can be attributed to a given situation, even though those involved somehow shared the same cultural and social universe. I realized that the fact that I was Black did not necessarily validate my presence as a researcher for them. They considered me part of the same universe of researchers who had previously taken them as objects of study.

The young people's attitude of refusal made sense to me when, in my search for other groups and collectives, I came across the same argument: we no longer want to be objects of research, we want to be active participants. During this journey, which lasted from August 2003 to August 2004, the growing importance of *hip-hop* culture was confirmed for me, and I expanded my knowledge of the diverse forms of the movement. The discoveries led to the possibility of working with activists from different groups, which would make it possible to look at the diverse configurations of *hip-hop*. For the continuity of the research since the first contact with the research subjects, I followed the premises of qualitative research adopted in literacy studies, which takes into account the existence of power relations and battles for socially legitimated positions concerning the use of writing from the first moments of contact with research subjects.

Considering that speech is dialogical by nature, the meetings were the spaces in which the utterances, always directed to another interlocutor, took on meaning, because the presence of the researcher contributes to the modification of the enunciative act (Amorim, 2004).

During the research process, a place, a gaze and a researcher's attitude were constructed. When working with subjects who have knowledge and meanings about things in the world — very different from the meanings I had attributed to them — it was necessary to construct a listening that embraced and interpreted the statements, guaranteeing an ethical and responsible attitude towards the individuals and their stories. My speech was one among many.

The portrait I managed to make of the group I was researching is a place of exotopy[62] and tensions due to the different positions and values between those who portray and those who are portrayed. Considering that the gaze of the researcher and the researched object is not coincidental, my task was to "try to capture something about the way they [the researched people] see themselves, then to fully assume my external place and from there to compose what I see about their views" (Amorim 2004, 14). It is an exercise I attempted to accomplish by bringing to bear the specificities of the literacy practices of the *hip-hop* movement.

Another aspect to consider is the researcher's responsibility to establish *what* the researcher sees and *how* they respond to what they see from their "singular and unique" position as a signature place. Because there is a difference of views and values in the commitment to communicate perceptions, it is equally essential that the subjects are aware of the readings that people make of them, since others already make those readings.

In a dialogical relationship, the researcher and the researched must assume that the different contexts in which people find themselves

---

6   Being able to see yourself through another's eyes.

are "an arena in which different values, generated in the different social positions we occupy, clash" (Amorim 2003, p. 19). In this sense,
one ought to understand this "as an event in which the difference
between values plays a fundamental role in the production of knowledge" (p. 18). Understanding this equation is fundamental so that
the occupation of different spaces does not necessarily imply sub-
jugation and hierarchies, but a space of exchange, negotiation and
learning.

THE CONSOLIDATION OF THE RESEARCH GROUP

A large number of the *rappers* with whom I made contact, who also
used the same arguments as the first group, were organizers, among
other activities, of the Hip-Hop Cultural Week, an event supported
by the NGO *Ação Educativa — Assessoria, Pesquisa e Informação*,[73]
to strengthen and give visibility to the cultural production of the
groups.

It was at one of these meetings in preparation for Hip-Hop Week,
at the beginning of July 2004, that I presented my research intentions to approximately 15 people. Most of them expressed strong
suspicion and disbelief about the project because of its academic nature. The first question came from Dimenor:

(...) when Analu said: I'm doing some stuff like this, like that, did
you see that I was the first one to say: it's just one more term paper
to be kept over there in the playboizada (rich kids) schoolbooks? I
was the first one to say that, bro, understand? that's when she turned
around and said: noooo:::::, I'm doing this, this and this... (Dimenor,
2004).

Dimenor's voice clashes with the voice of the academy anchored
in the positivist model of research which claims to be exempt from
relations with society. For Dimenor, academic work has no feedback
for the "objects" of research. It is a production directed to a certain
group with money and access to books: the "peers." This resistance

---

7   *Ação Educativa* is a non-governmental organization based in the central region of the City
of São Paulo. Since 1994 it has been developing and supporting projects in the areas of educational
rights and policies for youth, with the aim of influencing the formulation of public policy [www.acao-
educativa.org].

was directed against the academy as a whole, and against me as a researcher. Even though I am Black and have a background as an activist, I was still a researcher inserted into the academic universe. Dimenor's choice of words shows the different places that the researcher and the researched occupy: "*some stuff*" and "*playboizada*" [rich kids] symbolize his sarcastic view of the importance that the academy gives to a work that will only be accessible to a few people.

Although I replied, emphasizing that participation was voluntary and had no necessary link to the work developed during Hip-Hop Week or *Ação Educativa*, they reiterated the arguments of the first group I contacted:

- The works did not return to the movement;
- There was no socialization of the knowledge produced;
- In some cases, there was not even verbal feedback on the material generated in the field.

They said they were tired of being the object of research and, among other things, wanted me to explain their role in the work, the destination of the material and what the product would be.

The debate was productive as we planned a new meeting and, from it, several others in which the data were generated, through a mode of conducting research that was dynamic and tense, thus configuring itself as a space of learning and teaching for all of us.

From the first scheduled meeting, given the different locations and the tense power relations among the participants, the group made clear what their interests were:

1. Read and discuss materials about race relations;
2. Learn strategies for developing workshops;
3. Participate and give lectures in spaces other than those from *hip-hop*;
4. In addition to publishing articles and understanding a little more about how academic research is done, they wanted to expand their knowledge concerning the issues discussed.

In addition, and above all, they indicated that they would like the studies and analyses about themselves and other collectives from the *hip-hop* universe to be shared and disseminated with them.

SITUATIONS AND INSTRUMENTS FOR DATA GENERATION

The process of data generation was designed to rely on four research instruments: surveys, *rodas de conversa*, individual interviews and autobiographies. Eight meetings took place between June and December 2004. The data generated during these meetings, primarily the *rodas de conversa*, were audio recorded and some were photographed.

During the period of data collection, and also afterward, it was possible to observe the participation of young people in various activities, some of them motivated by our meetings, such as the preparation of lectures and workshops for young people, pedagogy students and teachers from the primary education system. In addition, during the meetings, the young people produced several newsletters, a wide range of documents and materials, such as newspaper articles about their work, fanzines they wrote, flyers for concerts and events, drafts of lyrics, personal notebooks, written projects, CDs and photographs.

It is important to point out that although we have generated a significant amount of data, we will focus our analysis on the *rodas de conversa* and a lecture the rappers gave to pedagogy students, as these give a perfect idea of the interactional situations that reflect literacy practices and identities under construction. The other data are important for a more accurate and detailed profile of these young people's relationship with the complex *hip-hop* movement.

The first tool I used was the surveys, intending to ascertain the socio-economic profile of the participants. They provided information about the living conditions and reading practices in which they were involved and allowed the identification of their collections. The questions were organized around areas or contexts considered relevant in our society: socioeconomic status; reading practices and collections; areas of coexistence and socialization. Other questions related to the capacity for self-analysis, asking them how they read, speak or write in different situations, or even about the performance of different activities and their frequency.

The surveys ended up raising the first issue discussed in the *rodas de conversa*. One of the young people, who had already demonstrated his autonomy and his ability to critique and reflect on materials and reading practices, scrapped the survey and added an item that he felt was missing to the proposed list of reading collections: the fanzine. After this first contact, full of resistance, I interviewed the young people individually while the collective meetings were taking place.

Both the interviews and the meetings, structured as *rodas de conversa*, took place at the headquarters of *Ação Educativa*. We occupied the meeting room of the executive secretary. All the participants were comfortably sitting on chairs around an oval table. The environment was generally quiet, and the meetings took place at night, between 7:00 and 10:00 pm.

Interviews served as an important strategy to generate data through a script of semi-structured questions that served as guiding themes for the dialogues. This technique mobilized informants to elaborate versions of their life histories and select events that they considered predominant in their trajectories as writing agents (Vóvio, 2007; Souza, 2005).

Another tool provided for the data generation process was autobiographies, which were generated unconventionally. By "autobiographies" I refer to the narratives they wrote about themselves that were not necessarily structured into a formal written statement. We agreed that they would write the autobiographies as homework, and everyone would read them in the next meeting. Three of the five participants did it.

The *rodas de conversa* consisted of six discussions, averaging two hours in length, on topics that involved the participants in an interactive process conducted with flexibility. The group agreed on the topics, usually as a way to follow up on an issue that had gained importance during the day. The topics were:

1. What they like to read;

2. Race relations in Brazilian society;

3. Autobiography - reading at home and school;

4. What is the importance of *hip-hop* in education?

5. The relationship between rap, reading and literature.

We created a space for discussion that, although focused on one topic, did not exclude the possibility of digressions and debates in an intense process of exchange.

The proximity between the researcher and the group, and between the group members themselves, did not mean that the tensions and conflicts in the interactions were relaxed. In the environment, there was a group of *rappers* who were a bit reluctant to accept talking about themselves and the world in the presence of a person from an academic environment. It was no longer a matter of meetings to organize some kind of movement-oriented activity, but rather a situation in which these socio-cultural experiences would be unveiled through language, revealing the trajectories of individuals with different histories.

Nevertheless, the dynamic, ironic and engaging style of the group shaped the meetings. I was constructing and taking on the interactions as a space for listening and talking. I tried to guide the circles as little as possible, as issues emerged amid controversial discussions. My interventions were just to mediate the discussions so that the different points of view could be exposed. For the group, the meetings gradually became a valued space for sharing, sociability and learning.

Image 1 — Research participants. Clockwise from top left— **Soneca** *(Jean Carlos Furio);* **Dimenor** *(Rodrigo de Oliveira Vicente);* **Débora** *Pavani Motta;* **LGe** *(Leandro Gomes) [squatting on the right] and* **Nathas** *(Jonata Marques de Oliveira) [squatting on the left].*

Five people — four men and a woman — signed the terms of commitment made by the "Teachers' Literacy" group and stayed for much of the work. Débora, who was preparing for the university entrance exam, participated irregularly in all the situations and applications of the instruments. The closest contact was with Dimenor, LGe, Soneca and Nathas.

From the beginning, they made it clear how they wanted to be called. The names above are the way they are known in the *hip-hop* universe, as MCs. When writing articles, they use their "real" names in parentheses. The question of self- naming is important because it relates to political choices, specifically new political identities taken on in the realm of social participation. Contrary to the theses of semantic theories for which names are merely labels, "one must think beyond the semantics of proper names to see the phenomenon of naming as an eminently political act" (Rajagopalan 2003, 82).

The collectives and musical groups, to which the participants in this research belong, show the same concern in defining their commitments and objectives. Dimenor and LGe belong to the group *Enraizados*, which has its headquarters in Rio de Janeiro and maintains relations with São Paulo and other states. The musical group they belong to is called *Submundo Racional*. Soneca and Nathas belong to the musical group *Lado Obscuro*. Débora introduced herself as one of the members of the collective *Só Pra Causar*, which is made up mainly of women and created specifically for the event *Semana do Hip-Hop* [Hip-Hop Week], since to participate it was required to belong to a collective or group.

THE ACTIVISTS' PROFILES

Débora — Black, 19 years old, high school graduate, single, lives in the Taboão da Serra, São Paulo. She gives lectures to groups discussing race relations and gender issues and participates in several activities related to the *hip-hop* movement.

Dimenor — Black, 25 years old, high school graduate, married, father of one child, office worker, lives in the region of Ipiranga. He writes, sings, has recorded several songs and represents the *hip-hop* movement within different institutions. He is an active participant in the movement.

Soneca — white, 29 years old, high school graduate, married, general assistant, lives in Ipiranga. He writes, sings, is a registered musician and participates in lectures and organizations with other *hip-hop* groups.

Nathas — Black, 19 years old, high school graduate, single, lives in the region of Ipiranga and works as a warehouse worker in a supermarket chain. Participates in the movement, sings and writes lyrics. Sometimes attends lectures. **LGe** — Black, 26 years old, high school graduate, resident of the East Zone - Cohab de Itaquera I, single. He is active in *hip-hop* and movements that deal with racial and youth issues. He composes *rap* lyrics and gives workshops and lectures on the movement.

Although it contains important data to measure the socio-economic and cultural profile of these young people, the profile presented says little about the complexity of any social identity of those from the "*periferia.*"

Themes that seem to be encapsulated in the formula "*periferia*" appear to be encapsulated in *rap* lyrics and the discourses of the movement: poverty, racism, discrimination, family relations and the importance of the *hip-hop* movement. To be from the *periferia* is to face social and racial discrimination, to have no access to quality public goods, to see "brothers" die or be arrested and to live the reality of unemployment, drugs and violence. In addition, the importance of the family in supporting themselves in the face of these adversities and, at the same time, looking for solutions, is evident. Participation in a movement like *hip-hop*, with resistance and transformation at its core, is essential to writing other histories.

Since the early 1970s in São Paulo, the precariousness of the *periferia* has fostered an alliance among the people who live there, placing them as protagonists in the processes of demanding improvements and rights. Today, living in the *periferia* means not only living in precariousness, but also being an agent of change. It is precisely the character and the form of the collective behavior of the inhabitants of the *periferia*, as well as their life dynamics, their political activities, their daily life and their forms of sociability characterized by problem-solving and resistance, that have given these spaces a different face. *Hip-hop*'s aphorism that the *periferia* is everywhere is a reflection of the fact that those who are most subjected to these social constraints are the youth. Social indicators relentlessly repeat that the most vulnerable social segment is young Black males. The data[8] also shows that cases of violence take place on a certain day and

---

8   Brazil has 34 million people between the ages of 15 and 24. Among these, 16 million are Black. For every homicide against whites aged 15 to 18, there are 2 deaths of Black people in the same age group. In 2000, 3,000 young Blacks and 1,800 whites died as victims of violence. Unemployment averages 34% for young Blacks and 28% for whites. Young Blacks between the ages of 15 and 18 in Brazil's metropolitan areas have an unemployment rate higher than the average for the total adult population: between 17% and 23%. Source: UNICEF (2005). E.N.: These statistics have exponentially worsened since former President Bolsonaro's administration. The period of Bolsonaro's presidency was 2019-2022.

at a certain time: usually in the *periferia*, on weekends and at night. These are the places where the young people who participated in this research live. I refer to the participants in this research as "young people" based on a broader socio-cultural concept of youth. In their narratives, the category of youth is not perceived as a homogeneous group characterized only by age, but also by other variables related to living conditions, racial belonging and community participation. It becomes necessary to understand the social category of youth as a cultural construction in its diversity.

Certain attitudes of the young people were constant, such as: arriving on time, bringing materials related to *hip-hop*, bringing information about cultural or political events that would take place in the city and writing down the dates and topics of discussion in their agendas. It seems to me that these attitudes are signs that the meetings gained density and importance for them. Throughout the meetings, I got closer to the group. The relationship we built was permeated by affectivity, commitment and tension.

During the research period, we organized ourselves to consider the reciprocity of the results of the work: for me, as a researcher, the end of my Ph.D. and a lot of stories to tell as an activist of the Black movement and educator; for them, the publication of an article on *hip-hop* and education and, subsequently, in December 2004, the creation of a working group called *Hip-Hop Educando [Educating with Hip-Hop]*. In their words, one of the effects of the research was to allow them to expand their understanding of their work and the educational potential of *hip-hop*.

As members of *Hip-Hop Educando*, they have experienced many moments that will be registered in their trajectory. Among them we have the participation as guest speakers at the final table of the 2006 *Congresso de Leitura* — COLE [Reading Conference] at UNI-CAMP [State University of Campinas]; the participation in training courses for teachers at the Project *Teia do Saber* and in a school of education; the participation in a DVD on the educational aspects of *hip-hop* by the State Secretary of Education for the project *Ensino Médio em Rede* in 2006; and a book on *hip-hop* aimed at young people.

We noticed the care with which the memory of the events was organized: folders with brochures, flyers, certificates, CDs and DVDs. These documents materialize what Gee (1990) classifies as portfolios: different ways that people manage, record and organize their curriculum, legitimizing the possession of knowledge. The importance lies in being able to demonstrate their trajectories in a world that demands they display their knowledge to keep meeting demand. For the activists, the research process and its results have been a business card for their identities and images built along the way.

CHAPTER 2

LITERACIES AND THE POLITICS OF REEXISTENCE IN DAILY LIFE

let's suppose in (discussion of) race[9] (.) so (.) I think it contributes a lot because like(.) one of the (.) characteristics of hip-hop, right (.) I don't know (.) it's rescuing our origins — (.) it is/ (.) it deepens:::s (.) why are we in that (.) in that situation/ (.) why do we have that (.) that condition, right (.) which is not another (.) I think it contributes to that right there (.) to wake up (.) it wakes up (.) that (.) curiosity (.) that debate (.) got it? (.) it awakens that right there.
(Nathas)

The theoretical perspectives presented here will allow me to analyze the singularities of literacy practices in *hip-hop* culture. I will discuss the postulates of the new studies on multiple and heterogeneous literacies (Street, 1984; Gee, 1990; Kleiman, 1995 2006a; Barton and Hamilton, 2000; Rojo, 2009), whose premises attach importance to the sociocultural perspective of language use practices. I will also present studies that, from a historical perspective, deal with aspects related to the education of the Black population in Brazil (Barros, 2005; Fonseca, 2005; Araujo e Silva, 2005; Cunha, 2005; Cardoso, 2005; Cruz, 2005; cf. also studies related to the education of the Black population in Brazil, especially after the enactment of

---

9   I emphasize that the expression "race" is far from the biological sense and exists as a social-historical construction. Therefore, it is effective and real only in the social world (Munanga, 2004).

Law 10.639/03[10]— which amends the LDB,[11] and includes the compulsory study of Afro-Brazilian history and culture in the official curriculum of public and private elementary schools in the country). I will then present the contributions of cultural studies, especially those of Hall (2003a, 2003b), which allow for a deeper discussion of the notions of culture and Black identities. Finally, I will highlight aspects of the Bakhtinian view of language that are fundamental to the discussion of literacies in *hip-hop*, since when language is considered social it proves productive for considering the particularities of discourses regarding the place and the position individuals occupy within a political framework and economic dynamics.

In accordance with the adopted concept of literacy, I reference the steps that compose the sociological method of analysis proposed by Voloshinov/Bakhtin ([1929] 1995). Prior to enunciation, it is necessary to deal with the forms and types of verbal interaction, in connection with the concrete conditions in which the ways of enunciating take place when tied with the dynamics of life and the ideological creations that enunciations present in verbal interactions.

To begin the discussion with the singularities of the social uses of written and inscribed language in the *hip-hop* universe, I take as valid the perspectives of new literacies studies, which understand literacy practices as multiple and historically situated. Far from being homogeneous, since they are culturally shaped and constructed, they are marked by heterogeneity and are related to the roles and social locations we occupy or are forced to occupy in society.

---

10   T.N.: Law 10.639/03 is a significant piece of legislation that was enacted on January 9, 2003. This law mandates the inclusion of African and Afro-Brazilian history and culture in the curriculum of Brazilian public and private schools. It is part of a broader effort to promote racial and ethnic diversity, combat racism and acknowledge the contributions of Afro-Brazilians to the country's history and culture. Key provisions of Law 10.639/03 include: inclusion of Afro-Brazilian history; racial and ethnic education; teacher training, as the law calls for the training of teachers to effectively implement these educational changes and incorporate Afro-Brazilian history and culture into their teaching materials and methods; recognition of cultural events; respect for religious freedom; curriculum integration — the content related to African and Afro-Brazilian history and culture should be integrated into various subjects across the curriculum, not just limited to history or social studies classes.

11   E.N.: Laws of Guidelines and Bases of Education [Leis de Diretrizes e Bases da Educação]: The LDB is considered to be the most important Brazilian law regarding education. This law was approved in December 1996 under the law number 9394/96; it was created to guarantee the right of the entire population to have access to free and quality education and to value education professionals, thereby charging Federal and State governments and municipalities with providing free public education.

Beyond literacy, the abilities to read and write can be better understood as "a set of social practices whose specific modes of operation have important implications for how individuals engaged in these practices build relations of identity and power" (Kleiman, 1995: 11). This conception forces us to consider the different values, functions and configurations that the phenomenon takes for different groups, depending on local contexts and specific cultural references, as well as on the structure that characterizes broader social processes.

Consider that the social and plural character of literacy practices validate practices acquired through both the schooling processes in more institutionalized spheres, and those acquired in learning processes and spaces in different spheres of everyday life (Barton & Hamilton 2000). We create ideas like these to understand the meanings attached to language, to the different modes of reading, writing and speaking that characterize the histories and trajectories of the literacies of different groups.

One of the hallmarks of *hip-hop* culture is the intimacy with which it combines and recombines multiliteracies in productions that mix oral, verbal, pictorial, analogical and digital media without hierarchizing them. This culture's universe takes into consideration both the educational practices shared by young people in the academic sphere, which do not always have precedents in their groups of origin, like those produced in the sphere of everyday life, that gives them meaning and objectives, and ownership of them. Moreover, *hip-hop* literacies are also supported by practices produced by Black social movements that have historically demanded rights, including in education.

I am interested in the elements that broaden our view of how we understand literacies in the plural. Especially when we consider the variables that are still little studied — race and gender — and, more, when we begin to look at these groups not paying attention to the absences, but to the presence of knowledge that is not socially valued, but important to their lives, as is the case of literacies within and from *hip-hop* culture.

My intention is to highlight the emergence of the *hip-hop* cultural movement as an agency of literacy[12] that shares commonalities with the various educational experiences of the Black social movement groups that preceded it. From this perspective, I attempt to describe the process through which *hip-hop* activists play a historical role in incorporating, creating, resignifying and reinventing the social uses of language, values and intentions of what I call Literacies of Reexistence [*Letramentos de Reexistência*].

When it comes to reading, writing and interpreting texts, or using literate orality, young people are not always considered autonomous users of written language according to school canons. Outside of school, however, there are other situations — even if they are not always recognized or authorized — that take place in the most diverse spheres of activity: at home, on the street, at work and in religious contexts. These are spaces that take on different meanings and present different ways to engage individuals or social groups. Therefore, literacies are multiple and, moreover, critical, since they encompass uses as diverse as the purposes of these practices.

The literacies of reexistence are unique because, by capturing the social and historical complexity that surrounds everyday practices of language use, they contribute to the destabilization of what can be considered crystallized discourses in which the socially validated practices of language use are only those taught and learned in formal institutions.

The values the young participants attributed to the use of reading and writing — while speaking about themselves — also recall the *hip-hop* movement and the literacies of resistance and reexistence that the Black population in Brazil has experienced for centuries.

The practices analyzed are established as reexistence since they suggest that young people should assume and maintain new social roles in their communities and those they are in contact with. Such a perspective contributes to thinking about necessary changes and to initiating changes in the broader processes and in different social

---

12   See Kleiman (2006b).

spheres,[13] such as the school, which still presents itself as exclusionary.

Literacies of reexistence here will be the reinvention of practices that activists carry out, referring to the matrices and traces of a history that is still little told, in which the use of language carries a history of contestation for formal and informal education. For *rappers*, education and the possession of the word are marked by the effort to recognize themselves, challenging, in different ways and different formats, the officially imposed subjection that still materializes in racism, prejudice and discrimination.

The uniqueness lies in the everyday micro-resistances re-signified in language, speech, gestures and clothing, not only in content but also in the way of speaking, which refers both to the dialogical nature of language and to the propositions of cultural studies that reveal that social identities, which are constantly being constructed, take place in a tense and contradictory way, typical of situations where socially legitimated spaces compete.

This perspective, which embraces and legitimizes the literacies of the *hip-hop* movement (Kleiman 1995, 1996b; Rojo 2009), because they are meaningful in terms of knowledge and rights, can also be productive for rethinking school literacies. The school is increasingly becoming the site of different cultures, although it is still unable to establish a dialogue — despite the fact that the need is already recognized — due to a process of exclusion that still marks the history of a Black and a white Brazil in terms of access, permanence and school success. Despite the changes, the country is still divided.

LITERACIES IN BLACK AND WHITE

Incredibly, it is still necessary to problematize the Eurocentric vision prevalent in the official history of public education in Brazil. Studies carried out by Barros (2005), Fonseca (2005), Araújo e Silva (2005), Cunha (2005), Cardoso (2005) and Cruz (2005) highlight the pro-

---

13   Spheres are understood as follows: "For the object, belonging to any sphere of reality, to enter the social horizon of the group and trigger a semiotic-ideological reaction, it is indispensable that it be linked to the essential socio-economic conditions of the said group, which concerns in some way the bases of its material existence" (Bakhtin, 1929: 45).

cess of slavery in our country and make important contributions to the analysis of the unequal ways in which the Black and white populations are integrated into the school universe.

The perverse effects of slavery, due to the social positions occupied or given in society, extend to the socio-cultural ways of using literacy and orality, as well as the meanings of these practices for white and Black people, even so long after the abolition of slavery.

In this sense, I bring to the center of narratives about schooling in Brazil some little-known tactics and strategies (De Certeau, 1994: 99) through which the Black population aims to self-educate, circumventing a series of more or less visible mechanisms of prohibition, experienced amidst negotiations and subversions, in confrontation with a historically unfavorable political, economic and cultural structure.

Barros (2005), in his research on education in São Paulo, shows that in Brazil, especially between the end of the 19th century and the beginning of the 20th century, there was a white action and a Black action, a segregationist process of schooling.

In the midst of this scenario, school writing, as well as some literacy practices closer to the European model and perspective, gained more visibility and legitimacy, to the detriment of the oral, self-generated and vernacular knowledge of the Indigenous and Black populations of African descent.

For part of the Black population, especially in the cities, schooling was seen as an opportunity for social and professional advancement. However, although the school was valued, it was often a place of exclusion and restriction for families; sometimes they stayed, even going through difficulties, and sometimes they dropped out. Although being away from the school environment was motivated by objective reasons, such as the need to work, some families removed or did not even enroll their children because they could not meet the requirements, which, according to the school documents of the time, included "appropriate clothing; the presence of a responsible adult for enrollment; in addition to the need to purchase school supplies and lunch." Failure to comply with these requirements led to embarrassment and dropping out.

As far as school integration was concerned, the newly liberated students[14] knew both the discourses in favor of their education — as a form of integration into the emerging class society — and those against their access. In their memories, humiliations and rejections appear as perhaps the most significant components that hindered insertion and permanence in school.[15]

According to the *Instrução Pública de São Paulo* [Public Instruction of São Paulo], there was anxiety about accepting the enrollment of Black children for fear that white families would refuse to keep their children in the institutions, fearing the proximity of socially inferior individuals. In society, as well as in the school, the presence of Black bodies and their core values of civilization, culture and beliefs, which were still unacceptable, triggered just as horrific a reaction as before the abolition of slavery. In this context, Black people were forbidden to learn to read and write because of the danger of "spreading education through the slave class" (Barros 2005, 84). Being literate could facilitate rebellion, insurrection and disobedience.

Moysés (1995) makes an important contribution to this discussion when he affirms that, in addition to the spatial rupture, Black people displaced from their homelands experience the dilution of their political and social organization, traditionally anchored in the oral culture.

Subjected to another language that undermined their cosmology, their ways of seeing the world and their preservation of histories and memories, they also lost their original place, the place of production of their own words (Moysés 1995, 56). Without mastering linguistic production, the word, which was also enslaved, is transformed not only into silence, "but into the absence of the word, the word as an ideological creation" (p. 56). In this context, where Portuguese is the official language, being white or Black is a decisive factor in

---

14   Slavery officially ended in Brazil in 1888, with slavery continuing into the early 20th century as the country transitioned into a post-enslavement economy.
15   The study by Barros (2005) and others shows that in the first decades of the 20th century, already in the period of the Brazilian Republic, the Black population had not removed the stigma of slavery that relegated them to an "inferior" category.

assigning value to an oral memory to be able to share, produce and transmit discourse with and about a particular history.

The deprivation of the legitimacy of the language, of the African oral word, represents on the one hand a break with its ethnic identity and on the other hand a first confrontation with the culture of the European written language. There are ruptures, negotiations and confrontations, each with new prohibitions and restrictions. The use of oral and written language is clandestine, and it is in this dynamic that the appropriations and uses of oral and written language take place.[16] Being a white reader differs from being a Black reader because, for Black people, being a reader is inscribed in a double trajectory that is not conducive to maintaining their identity as readers. Alternatively, there is the representation that, as inferior and savage, Black readers must be civilized in order to be able to be a reader; on the other hand, coming from orality and accessing different reading in the diverse environments where it circulated, the Black population creates what Moysés (1995, 60) classifies as a "pre-knowledge of writing" that does not lead to an identification with reading or being a reader. To be a reader, within a process in which the written word is European and responds to current racist theories, I need to become white. The readings made by Black and mixed-race people, which are strongly influenced by the devalued oral tradition, together with their bodies of African descent, have no place, no value compared to the values of reading and writing taught in school or outside of it.

According to Moysés (1995), before abolition the official indexes indicated that there was one literate person for every thousand enslaved people. Slaves who learned to read and were statistically recorded as literate were few because the measurements could not capture the other forms of appropriation of reading and writing that occurred in a clandestine way, as well as the various cultural practices mediated through the use and circulation of printed materials in different communicative situations.

Within this literate world, contact with writing generally maintained links with enslavement: listening to texts mediated by the

16   Notably, there was also a large contingent of illiterate poor whites. Given this scenario, the existence of unsystematic learning of writing, which took place outside the school environment and was often diffuse, also stands out. However, whites were not aware of the official prohibition imposed on Black people.

voice of a white person, accompanying movements of reading and religious images, and later in urban spaces in which commerce led them to count. Knowing that silent and individual reading and writing were not for them led to the understanding that the European language created a non-place in society, isolating them in every way, especially through the prohibition of accessing a school education.

The literacy rates of the time, anchored in the relationship between schooling and literacy as socially legitimized in academic space, reveal little or nothing about the cultural practices, re-creations and uses of an oral or written language by enslaved or free Black people. Being attentive to cultural forms requires an understanding of the different ways in which different social and cultural groups view the process of literacy.

For Hall (2003) as well as for Gilroy (2001), African peoples enter different scenarios carrying in their bodies an ancient construct — knowledge, words, art, musicality, aesthetics, values — sources of rites and political, cultural and social practices that supported them in their diverse ways of reinventing life during the process of enslavement.

The multiple configurations that Black African culture assumes outside the African continent are important because they assert that when people are displaced from the Africas and come into contact with other social subjects — Asian and European cultures — they are forced to confront strange and humiliating realities and, in the face of them, are forced to create a series of strategies to sustain life in the dynamisms of daily life. Over time, Black cultural productions, "cultures of resistance," before being understood in their "purity" as a preservation or a re-turn to the traditions or legacies of "Africa,"[17] are hybrid productions born at the crossroads of cultures as combinations of transgressions, submissions, negotiations, prohibitions, exchanges, ruptures and subversions.

---

17   Hall (2003) points out that the term "Africa" is a modern construct, constructed and incapable of revealing the diverse ethnicities, groups, cultures and languages brought together by the slave trade (p. 30). In fact, it was created to refer to "those who came from Africa" without regard to ethnic characteristics.

The same is true for Brazil, where the Black segment of the population, silenced but not passive, continues to work in the marginal spaces, a tactical position so that the *"tactics"* [*golpes astutos*] (De Certeau, 1994) can be delivered at opportune moments because one is neither weak nor strong all the time.

For Black people, cultural production can be seen as supporting ways of "seeking freedom" in a social context that chose to dehumanize them, to transform them into things; "[a]rt has become the backbone of the political cultures of the enslaved and their cultural histories" (Gilroy, 2001: 129). In the universe of art, music was central, materialized in styles such as blues, jazz and soul that would later influence *rap* and, more generally, *hip-hop* culture.[18]

Given that in a particular culture there is not just one literacy, but multiple literacies associated with different spheres of life, as well as a diversity of ways in which individuals participate in events and situations in these spheres, it is relevant to investigate the paths through which these subjects, located in specific contexts, as members of specific communities, have moved in the universe of schooling.

Studies by Fonseca (2005), Araújo e Silva (2005), Cunha (2005), Cardoso (2005) and Cruz (2005), emphasize the existence of a wide range of actions and institutions of the Black movement in favor of schooling for the Black population, with greater intensity in the 20th and 21st centuries. They highlight, among other historical examples, the activities of the Brazilian Black Front — *Frente Negra Brasileira* (FNB) in the 1930s and the Experimental Black Theater — *Teatro Experimental do Negro* (TEN) in the 1940s, institutions that, among other cultural and political activities, maintained literacy classes for uneducated Black adults in their places of operation.

Educational activities in the most diverse spaces (homes, churches, academic centers) established themselves as spaces for the creation and support of projects for cultural and political purposes. They gave impetus to current institutions and actions, such as the Black Researchers Congress — *Congresso de Pesquisadores Negros* (COPENE), which brings together researchers working on the theme

18   Blues, jazz and soul were born in the working world before the abolition of slavery and accompanied Black men and women in Protestant churches. Later, the genres were transformed and entered the phonographic market.

of race relations; the Association of Black Researchers — *Associação de Pesquisadores e Pesquisadoras Negros/as* (ABPN), which brings together scholars from all over Brazil, and the Afro-Brazilian Study Centers — *Núcleos de Estudo Afro-brasileiros* (NEABs). These spaces are the site of literacy practices. They must be understood as the space where the people produce social actions, amidst the power relations, intentions and conflicts of the different subjects that compose them.

Nourished by these practices, *hip-hop* groups dedicated to education maintain organizational principles, and also constitute self-education groups that aim to seek and take ownership of knowledge for their members. *Hip-hop* shows itself as a *reinventor of traditions*, recreating in a unique way the cultural and educational practices that have characterized the Black social movement in different eras since the arrival of Black Africans in Brazil. They address literacies as social practices that, in addition to individual language use skills, take place in specific contexts: social, political and cultural. The young people involved in this research talk about themselves and about *hip-hop* culture, but also about Black culture and identity.

TODAY'S DATA: THE BLACK POPULATION IN THE LITERATE UNIVERSE

In the midst of a situation of accelerated social and economic transformations, the slogan "Education for All"[19] became a slogan present in the discourses of educators and politicians, especially since 1990 when the country made a series of commitments related to guaranteeing the right to education for all children, adolescents and adults. In line with the legal framework, schooling, identified as a condition for equity, has gained space in government agendas and has begun

19   The World Conference on Education for All was held in Jomtien, Thailand, from March 5 to 9, 1990. On that occasion, the participating countries committed themselves to expanding the conditions of access to education as a right by signing the official document, the World Declaration on Education for All. The first article, on the goals, states, "Every person - child, adolescent or adult - must be able to benefit from educational opportunities designed to meet his or her basic learning needs. These needs include both the essential learning tools (such as literacy, numeracy and problem-solving) and the basic learning content (such as knowledge, skills, values and attitudes) necessary for human beings to survive, develop their full potential, live and work with dignity, to participate fully in development, to improve the quality of their lives, to make informed choices and to continue learning. The extent of basic learning needs and the ways in which they are met vary from country to country and culture to culture and inevitably change over time." Source: (http://www.brasilia. unesco.org, accessed May 2009).

to receive investments, so that proposals formulated in dialogue with state and municipal authorities and various segments of civil society have expanded their expressiveness and local character.

The effort to implement changes in education can be seen, for example, in the investments made in the initial and continuing training of education professionals and in the increase in the channels for civil society's participation in school management, in order to encourage the development of political-pedagogical projects that change the daily life of schools.

Nevertheless, despite the progress made in the Brazilian educational system, there is still much to be done in order to implement an education that proves capable of concretely welcoming all differences with equal rights, in order to confront the forms and mechanisms of exclusion that still prevent the school from being a space of justice.

Today's school receives different subjectivities inscribed in the life stories of its actors. However, some values and principles are not always appropriate for understanding differences. Inequality is a reality experienced by different individuals according to aspects of identity — class, gender, ethnicity, region, individuals according to aspects of identity — class, gender, ethnicity, region, sexuality, race — that socially hierarchizes and diminishes certain groups. However, the lack of equality is more acute for people of African descent, whose phenotypic characteristics are still a cause of prejudice and discrimination, not always verbally explained, but reported in several educational surveys. Data from the 2007 school census, analyzed in 2008 by the Institute of Applied Economic Research — *Instituto de Pesquisa Econômica Aplicada* (IPEA),[20] reveals the lack of equity when it shows that among white youth aged 15 to 17, 70% had completed primary school, while only 30% of Black young people had done so. In high school, 62% of young whites between 15 and 17 years old were in school, while the percentage of Black people in the same age group was 31%. Looking at the 19-year-old group, 55% of whites graduated high school, while only 33% of Blacks did the

---

20   Racial Disparities, Racism, and Public Policy: 120 years after abolition. Brasília: Institute for Applied Economic Research, 2008. Available at: <www.ipea.gov.br/sites/000/2/ pdf/08_05_13_120 anos Abolição V colectiva.pdf>. (Theodoro org.)

same. In addition, 12.6% of the white population over the age of 25 have a university degree, compared to 3.9% of Black people.

The numbers are also not encouraging, as shown by Paixão (2008), when analyzing the educational profile of the Black population in the educational system, from 1995 to 2006, alongside unfavorable indicators concerning both the Portuguese and mathematics proficiency tests in the *Sistema Nacional de Avaliação da Educação Básica* — SAEB [the National System of Basic Education Evaluation], regarding the high rate of age-grade gaps. Surveys from the early grades to higher education show irregular paths, dropouts and school expulsion, in contrast to the greater number of Black people in youth and adult education. This shows that as the years of schooling advance, fewer Black people remain in school.

The following table shows the percentage distribution of illiteracy by color or race, according to the Brazilian Institute of Geography and Statistics — *Instituto Brasileiro de Geografia e Estatísticas* (IBGE), for the year 2007:

Table 1 — Illiteracy rate of people aged 15 and over (%) (2007)

Large regions, federation units and metropolitan regions	Total	Color or Race		
		White	Black	Pardos[21]
Brazil	10.0	6.1	14.3	14.1
North	10.8	7.5	14.7	11.7
Northeast	19.9	15.3	23.1	21.7
Southeast	5.7	4.1	9.4	7,.9
South	5.4	4.4	9.9	9.4
Mid-west	8.1	5.4	14.5	9.3

Source: IBGE, National Household Sample Survey 2007.

---

21   T.N.: According to the Brazilian Institute of Geography and Statistics (IGBE), the Black population in Brazil is formed by people who self-define as preta/o (literally "Black," usually used by those who are dark-skinned) or as *parda/o*. The term *pardo* is used by IBGE to refer to mixed-race people. Historically, the idea of *pardo* as an ethnic group emerged in Brazil during the colonial period. E.N.: *Pardo* functions as a non-white Afrodescendant category in which folks can disidentify with Blackness, or who are raised as non-Black. People who identify as *pardos/as* have to deal with anti-Black racism, as shown by Table 1, whether they personally recognize it as racism, or identify with Blackness.

The indices related to instruction by race/color reveal, according to a document referring to the city of São Paulo,[22] that:

Among the population aged 10 years or more, the percentage of Black people with no access to education or less than 1 year of school education is almost double related to whites. At the highest levels of schooling, the situation is reversed — among those with 10 or 11 years of schooling, the percentage of Black people is 25 percent lower than whites, and among those with more than 12 years of schooling, it is almost 80 percent lower (p. 16).

The same situation of inequality persists at the national level. These figures are indisputable; inequalities in years of schooling persist between Blacks and whites in the school environment. For our investigation, two aspects are currently important that have served to fuel the debate about the causes of racial inequalities in schooling: economic inequality, which generates poverty,[23] and racial inequality, which has its origins in the process of constituting the Brazilian nation. In 2004, the poorest 10% of Brazilians accounted for 0.9% of the national income; the poorest 20%, 2.8%; the richest 20%, 61.1%; and the richest 10%, 44.8%.[24]

In addition to the profound inequality between rich and poor, access is always filtered through race. The following tables show the income distribution between the white population and the Black or *parda* population (according to the classification adopted by IBGE). It should be noted that the white population represents 49.4% and

---

22   Data analyzed by the Fundação de Sistema de Análise de Dados [Data Analysis System Foundation] — SEADE — made available by the Instituto Brasileiro de Geografia e Estatística — IBGE [Brazilian Institute of Geography and Statistics] in 2003.

23   Pochmann is one of those scholars for whom the definition of poverty has a subjective dimension, since the criteria for defining what society considers necessary for a dignified life vary from moment to moment, and even if it is possible to assign values and measure what determines the poverty line by means of income thresholds, new needs are created. Moreover, he writes, "In an increasingly complex society, new forms of exclusion are emerging that are not related to low income, forcing a rethinking of the criterion of social exclusion in order to capture, in a more comprehensive way, the various forms of precariousness or lack of access to a set of social goods, thereby encompassing the inequalities that appear in different forms" (Pochmann 2004, 66-7).

24   Information from the Human Development Report 2007/2008. Data refer to income shares by population percentiles, sorted by income per capita.

Blacks and *pardos* 49.7% of the total Brazilian population, estimated at 189,820,000 in 2007.[25]

Table 2 — Distribution, per capita, of monthly family income for persons aged 10 and over with earned income among the poorest 10% of all persons, by color or race (%) (2007)

White	Black or *Pardos*
25.4	74.0

Source: IBGE, National Household Sample Survey 2007.

Table 3 — Distribution, per capita, of monthly family income for persons aged 10 and over with earned income among the richest 1% of all persons, by color or race (%) (2007)

White	Black or *Pardos*
86.2	12.1

Source: IBGE, National Household Sample Survey 2007.

There are also differences between men and women. In 2007, the average number of years of education among women over 15 was 7.4, while the average for men was 7.1. Despite having more education than men, women receive lower wages, as shown in the table below.

Table 4: Income of people considering family arrangement by sex (2007)

Men		Women	
The per capita proportion that have up to half a minimum salary (usually monthly minimum salary) (%)		The per capita proportion that have up to half a minimum salary (usually monthly minimum salary) (%)	
Up to 1/2	2 or more	Up to 1/2	2 or more
25.8	21.1	29.2	19.1

Source: IBGE, National Household Sample Survey 2007.

It is a very complex socio-economic context that indicates the predominance of inequalities for an immense population distributed

---

25   Brazilian Institute of Geography and Statistics — IBGE, National Household Sample Survey 2007. E.N.: At the time of this translation, the Black population (Black and pardo/a/e) of Brazil had grown to 53% of the nation.

over a vast territory. In line with the position defended by sectors of Black social movements, racial inequality, as part of a socio-historical construction, cannot be analyzed in isolation from economic and social inequalities. From this perspective, the poverty argument is insufficient as the main reason for the proportionally greater exclusion of Blacks from schooling. However, it can be taken as part of the explanation if we consider that, to use an expression of Paixão (2008), "poverty in Brazil has a color: Black" (p. 18), as it is also printed in the data of IBGE. In Paixão's (2008) studies, data on racial inequalities have served to broaden the possibilities for understanding the category of poverty beyond access to material goods, to also understand it "from the point of view of the possession of immaterial assets, such as the right to education, the protection of life,[26] as well as the validity of collective claims at the political level" (p. 18). Although there are poor people of different colors, ethnicities or races, or even Black men and women with higher incomes, the reasons for the existence of poverty are not the same for different groups. For the Black segment, he asserts, the main cause of poverty is the persistence of racism, prejudice and racial discrimination, which do not help Black people with greater purchasing power or higher levels of schooling to access spheres of importance, such as the university. In the same vein, Santos (2003) argues that racism and discrimination perpetuate the vicious cycle of exclusion that the Black population has sought to fight against over the centuries, including in the educational sphere.

Data from the study by Abramovay (2005, 564) point out that dropouts — either the student who drops out of school or the school that drops the student — or failures and flops at school have explanatory links with the peculiar racism experienced in Brazil, whose diversified mechanisms do not segregate or prohibit, but generate asymmetries and disadvantages that fall mostly on the Black segment of the population.

---

26   "Victims of Violence Have Age, Social Class and Color" is the title of an article published in the magazine Mundo Jovem, which publishes data from the 2008 Map of Violence in Brazilian Municipalities, which shows that between 1996 and 2006, the homicide rate of the young population had an increase of 31.3%, while the percentage in the total population was 20%. Diving into the data on youth mortality, the article states: "Poverty has a color, and in Brazil it is Black. Blacks have a victimization rate 73.1% higher than whites in the total population and 85.3% higher among the youth" (p. 11, <www.mundojovem.com.br>, accessed May 2009).

The reasons for not staying in school include: the differences in treatment and distribution of affection in relation to Black and white children; the scarcity of teaching materials that positively address African and Afro-Brazilian history and cultures; and the minimal importance attributed to conflicts involving nicknames and jokes, and even silencing and fear in the face of the *negro* or *preto* "namings," which configures a drama in the daily life of the school environment. The fact is that racial inequality persists in Brazilian society. The figures show that the school system is at a disadvantage, which, despite some changes, keeps the average number of years of study between Blacks and whites[27] barely changed. According to Henriques (2001), the average number of years of study for white adults is 6.6, while the average for Black adults is 4.4. At the beginning of the 21st century, the difference of more than two years is practically the same as at the beginning of the previous century, so it can be assumed that there is still a white Brazil and a Black Brazil (Henriques, 2001: 20). The educational system has, however, progressed in terms of democratizing access for all.

The set of affirmative actions beginning to take shape in Brazilian society is directed precisely against the division of Brazil, claiming equality also in the field of education.

CULTURES, IDENTITIES AND INTERSECTIONS IN LANGUAGE

In order to engage *hip-hop* literacies, it is interesting to think about the confluence of the notions of culture and identity (Hall 2003) as two concepts that move in the field of negotiations, elaborations and re-elaborations according to the engagements and places where socio-historical subjects circulate.

For Hall (2003), the cultural terrain, understood as a battleground for meanings, becomes even more tense and contested when the rapid transformations of societies weaken local narratives, leading to the displacement of old hierarchies. In these contexts, diversified

27   Investment in the discourse on the richness of cultural diversity does not yet translate into access to the distribution of material and immaterial goods. Contestation will be one of the ubiquitous themes in the conversations analyzed in Chapters 4 and 5. The analyses will make it possible to follow the battles, and the struggles for the fixation of meaning, which can be perceived through the expressiveness and valuation that words like "diversity," "racism," "Blackness" and "whiteness" gain in verbal interactions.

social practices force us to conceive the emergence of new ways of perceiving and validating popular and everyday practices.

In this scenario of struggle for ideas and meanings, in the midst of homogenizing cultural projects, "marginality" opens gaps in the search for ways to gain more space in society. With the transformations resulting from the history of struggles and claims for the right of "different differences" to exist, new subjects emerge, and new identities are produced in a flow marked by "positional wars" in the cultural scene; confrontations occur between dominant and dominated sectors that, without leaving the intricate game of power relations, redefine culture and alter the balance of cultural hegemony (Hall, 2003: 338-9).

The analysis of the new contours that culture acquires demands understanding it as a struggle, as a field of actions, as acts and situations that, in the historical process, assume different forms. It is in the social dynamics that the elements of different traditions meet and "can be reorganized to articulate different practices and positions and acquire a new meaning and relevance" (Hall, 2003: 260). The new meanings are part of a process of change that different cultures go through. In this sense, Black culture is no longer understood as something static and unified, immutable, endowed with essentiality, but rather as a system of meanings in permanent change.

The terrain of culture and tradition is understood as the intersection of different ideas and interests, and the conflicts and tensions arising from the clash of forces can be understood as raw material for the appropriations and negotiations in which sectors of social minority groups engage. These are appropriations and negotiations that interfere with, and sustain the construction of, social identities. In this way, if Black popular culture, as well as others that are socially marginalized, gains the contours of a local character, of contradictions, of contestation and negotiation, it cannot be analyzed or bundled by arguments sustained in simple binary oppositions: Black/white, high/low, authentic/ inauthentic, pure/impure. One must consider the paths taken by the cultures, forming routes and re-creations that sometimes return to their own communities of origin to be recreated again.

The notion of cultures, far from embracing anachronism and "purity," becomes the space in which transformations take place as a result of the struggles of domination and resistance, constituting political and social relations over time. In this way, cultures do not end up as an immutable stratum, absolutely encapsulated by the forms of the dominant culture. The field of culture is set:

> in the complex lines of resistance and acceptance, refusal and capitulation, which transform the field of culture into a kind of permanent battlefield, where definitive victory is not obtained, but where there are always strategic positions to be conquered or lost (Hall, 2003: 255).

The decentering of culture can open paths to new spaces of contestation, to new ways of acting in the gaps of a social and economic situation. Understood as always being in transformation, in culture there is no passivity, there are always negotiations and confrontations. There are interpretations and reinterpretations, more or less visible or invisible through different mechanisms, that inform a process of hybridization, an important issue when focusing on the situated speech of activists in the *hip-hop* cultural movement.

I borrow the concept of hybridization from Canclini (2005), who understands it as "sociocultural processes in which discrete structures or practices that exist separately combine to produce new structures, objects, and practices" (Canclini 2005, XIX). This concept, used with multiple meanings, is gaining relevance in the social sciences and other fields of knowledge that seek to grasp the complex relationships that are established amid socio-political and cultural configurations. Considering hybridization as an incessant and multiple process of the fusion and recombination of structured social practices, it is essential to situate such practices in socio-historical contexts. They are always shaped by asymmetrical power relations in which references touch, clash and merge. From this perspective, identities can no longer be seen as a set of fixed characteristics or endowed with an essence, whether of race or ethnicity, but as complex productions that are always in flux.

The concept of hybridization makes it possible to question the essentialist discourses of identity, authenticity and cultural purity, showing the possibilities of negotiations, conflicts and alliances — more or less enduring — present in the tense arrangements that occur at the intersections that generate multiple cultural processes.

By entering the social structures and participating in the power relations embedded in our social practices, there is no permission to separate ourselves from the plural and be only one (Hall, 2003). In this sense, looking at the identities that *rappers* mobilize in interactions brings with it the need to understand them as always in a process, within speech, as a "way of constructing meaning that influences and organizes both our actions as well as our sense of ourselves" (Hall, 2003: 50). What it means to be an educated, young, Black *rapper* from the *periferia*, is rooted in identities that are established and shaped in the function, and in the presence, of the other.

> The Black label is, thus, an example not only of the political character of the new identities, that is, of their positional and conjunctural character (their formation in and for specific times and places), but also of the way in which identity and difference are inextricably articulated or intertwined in different identities, one never completely annulling the other (Hall, 2003: 68).

Like culture and traditions, identity is increasingly recognized in its multiple dimensions and in its different negotiated and possible contours: who is male, female, young, from the center,[28] from the *periferia*, white, Black. In this sense, even though one can contemplate a core identity in the subject, it is formed and transformed discursively, in social interaction. Thus, "ideas and concepts do not occur, neither in language nor in thought, in that single and isolated way, with its contents and references irrevocably fixed" (Hall, 2003: 286), but in dialogues, in exchanges that inform not the identity, but the identities of the subjects.

One of the important dimensions in the process of identity constitution is to understand speech as a form of social action, through which people, in interaction, act towards each other, as can be seen in the formulations of Bakhtin and his circle.

---

28   E.N.: In the geographical context of Brazilian cities, people who are wealthier live closer to the center of the city, while poor people live further away from the city centers.

BAKHTINIAN ASSUMPTIONS OF LANGUAGE

Taking as a basis the dialogical conception of language, which ultimately postulates that there is no language without individuals, plural individuals, who impregnate language with their ideologies and social practices, show how language can be understood only in the social instances of use, which necessarily implies considering the ideological content in the enunciations. From such a perspective, even individual mental thought, which results from the ideology of everyday life, understood as "the totality of mental activity centered on everyday life" (Bakhtin/Voloshinov 1995 [1929], 118), influences and is influenced by the "constituted ideological systems" that surround the subject in society. The word, which is given in the measure of the encounter with the other and with the concrete situation, intervenes in the utterances.

Being of a social and ideological nature, words reveal themselves and gain meaning in concrete interactions, when shared socially, in conversation between two or more individuals inserted in the flow of daily communication. The word is always addressed to another subject; it is always a response to someone based on the assumption of the social horizon informed by aspects shared by both the speaker and the listener. It is in the interaction that language sets itself in motion and provokes response actions in relation to the word. The meaning of the word is projected in the relationship between the interlocutors and determined by the contexts, which can be multiple and varied. In this case, it is in the dialogic clash between the process of listening and understanding that the understanding of the spoken word or lived experience takes place.

The concept of active and responsive comprehension is fundamental to understanding the complex game that is established in the universe of *hip-hop* culture, which, by excellence, is a place where the enunciators maintain a relationship with other voices that, in the movement back and forth, work on the construction of meanings. The way language manifests itself in *hip-hop* culture problematizes the accommodation of views concerning social contradictions, in addition to showing other ways of thinking about the place of wisdom, knowledge and of values such as solidarity and collectivity. It is flagrant how *rap* presents itself, within *hip-hop* culture, as one of the most expressive elements for the perception of movement in Bakhtin's responsive word.

It is within the scope of the manifestation possibilities of dialogism that polyphony can be understood as the conflicting relationship that my word maintains with the other's word.

The expression of the word, unrepeatable, and always unpublished, is not in the word itself, it is not born with the word, but it becomes alive in the contact, in the friction with the concrete reality realized by the enunciation, which is individual, but not detached from the ideologies that surround speaker and listener. The crossing, tense and conflictive tone of these voices is the basis that sustains the permanent dispute for meanings present in *rap* lyrics:

> *Rap* is intensely, exuberantly dialogic. (...) emerges from a dialogical process: from the conversation between members of a group that interact in close physical proximity: they look each other in the eye, exchange verses, homages or insults, and, in general, "feed on the intensity of each other" (Stam, 1992: 75-6).

Another approximation to be established between aspects of Bakhtinian theory and the *hip-hop* universe lies in the notion of verbal interaction. Considering that, in society, words circulate by word of mouth, they belong to everyone and no one. They come to life in each unique enunciation, which takes on different forms, depending on the aspects that conform to the situation and the context involving the interlocutors. In this perspective of language, the word is always dependent on social evaluation, on the lens through which the interlocutors evaluate themselves.

The conception of language use in Bakhtin's circle, emerging from concrete enunciative needs, provides an argument for understanding the enunciative play of *hip-hop* activists in various situations in which they demonstrate that "without evaluative accent, there is no word" (Bakhtin/Voloshinov, 1995 [1929]: 132). In this case, it is important to know both the verbal and the non-verbal context, that is, who the interlocutors are, and what place and social position they occupy in the context of political and economic dynamics, since the movements of someone who speaks are considered in the function of the listener — the gestures, hands and eyes are also placed in the function of the audience. It should also be taken into account that enunciations are constructed in relation to certain roles and positions that those involved play in a given enunciative situation, roles that are also more or less valued according to the social and historical space in which individuals and their social practices are inserted.

Every use of the word involves human action in relation to someone, in a specific interactional context, in which the search for appropriation occurs, the battle for words and their meanings and the dispute of social identities. The dialogical relations of reexistences are also configured in a process that involves negotiation, reinvention and subversion of asymmetrical power relations. No matter how simple a statement is, it is always addressed to someone and carries a position, an action in the face of the reality in which we live.

Being in *hip-hop* brings the possibility of approaching discursive practices that allow one to get clues, information to understand one's own life and the life of one's group of belonging. In Nathas's words, *why do we have this (.) this situation, right? (.) which is not another (.) I think it contributed to that (.) to awaken (.) it awakens (.) this (.) curiosity (.) this debate (.) got it? (.) it awakens that.*

For Nathas and the other participants in this research, the ways in which words are used are important because they engage in the re-signification of contemporary issues, including racial and social issues. In the debate — replication — the words take on meaning beyond the four expressions of graffiti, dance, sound and poetry that characterize *hip-hop* culture.

CHAPTER 3

HIP-HOP: A CULTURAL PRODUCTION OF THE BLACK DIASPORA

(hip-hop) incorporated from Movements /.../ from the Movements over there (.) incorporated, right/ formed the hip-hop Movement with those elements/ it is from then on that they started to attract young people and everything else, right,/ what hip-hop is made of (.) because it's no use going up to the guy and asking if it started with hip-hop/ it's what he's doing in hip-hop, right, bro/ (.) it's doing good for the Movement / where it (hip-hop) came from, we know it didn't start, right,/ there are the little (.) lying stories that we see around, right,/ like that little talk about hip-hop about hip-hop not from rap (.) that rap started as a form of protest/ (.) we know this is +not true/ how it started.

This chapter explains the trajectories of the *hip-hop* movement, which are fundamental to understanding how interactions carried out in a continuous flow of contacts mark the culture in two ways: as a diasporic production, informed by traces of culture and histories of African matrices that are locally re-signified, and as a cosmopolitan movement in dialogue with modern urban and literate technologies. Approaching the situations of historical production and the characteristics of the field of culture as a space for making politics is essential in order to understand not only the content but also the forms of the statements that I will analyze in the following chapters, according to the sociological method of analysis proposed by Voloshinov/Bakhtin ([1929] 1995).

I briefly deal with aspects related to the origins of *hip-hop* in Jamaica and the United States to later focus on its emergence, development and transformations in São Paulo.

Although it is not possible to accurately describe *hip-hop* through a single version, one of the most important lines of thought claims that the phenomenon consolidated as a culture and gained social and political recognition from its emergence in the New York neighborhoods of the 1980s, when it took on social and artistic contours. Authors such as Gilroy (2001), Hall (2003), and Canclini (2005) agree that there is no single history of *hip-hop*. As a cultural movement, it transforms itself in the different contexts in which it arrives, hybridizing and taking on different formats, resignifying in different ways the effects of the phenomenon of a Black diaspora around the world, making musicality one of the sustaining elements of its social, cultural and political organization.

For Black people, musical culture has been "both the production and the expression of this transvaluation of all values that the history of racial terror in the New World has precipitated" (Gilroy, 2001: 94), providing the basis for the constitution of their subjectivities and a Black culture and identity, not only in the United States but also in other parts of the world. It is not without reason that *hip-hop* is best known for histories in which the confrontation of social prohibitions and restrictions takes place through the articulation of forms of resistance through language, the use of the body and art.

HIP-HOP BREAKS DOWN ROUTES OF DISCONTINUITY INTO NEW CONNECTIONS

Lindolfo Filho's (2004) ideas help us think about aspects of the emergence of *hip-hop* culture in Jamaica, which was going through a "period of high unemployment and a severe government crisis." Social and racial problems "were the triggers of various currents and trends in rap, in which social criticism and the orality of African culture were the tonics" (Lindolfo Filho, 2004: 138). Between 1920 and 1930, the Jamaican capital began to receive a large contingent of young Black and poor people who migrated from the countryside to the city. Faced with an unfavorable conjuncture, these boys, the rude boys, without professional placement and with little schooling, made daily life lived on the streets both a space of sociability and a possibility of advancement through music:

> Creating songs that spoke about everyday life was one of the only options for these young people, who usually led a very risky life, and generally a very short one, in transit between misery and violence. For a rude, the only way to get rid of the neighborhoods of West Kingston was a hit single [album with only one or two songs by the artist] or a police officer shot (Lindolfo Filho, 2004: 132).

The urban environment allowed the rude boys to create a lifestyle in which the use of language was aimed at talking about everyday experiences and marking positions of contestation against what society was trying to institute for them: "Black," from the country, "ignorant" and without professional specialization. One of their characteristics was telling stories about life, talking about painful issues through improvised songs in sermons, orientations and words that could make people believe in the possibility of facing and overcoming problems. The celebrations, which took place in the most remote and poor neighborhoods, began to be frequent. The innovative way of accompanying the sound of the turntables and the swaying bodies, all embryonic *hip-hop* practices, stood out. At the same time, in the 1960s, Jamaica, which was experiencing a series of social and political problems, was also the scene of the emergence and development of Black activist groups for rights and social justice, which, together with the principles of the Rastafarian movement, defended, among other things, the emancipation of the Black population. Drawing on sources in the African tradition, Rastafarianism "established a new way of reading the Bible, subverting it, and playing a crucial role in the modern movement that made Jamaica and other Caribbean societies 'Black' for the first time and irrevocably so" (Hall, 2003: 43). Before going global, Rastafarian doctrine and discourse gradually permeated the lyrics of reggae singers and greatly influenced the experiences of *rude boys*.

> In the midst of the Jamaican *reggae* movement, party enter-tainers added to the sounds of the turntables recreations of rhythmic lines and, over them, another spontaneous speech, that is, the *talk over* [talk over (or on) above]. Hence, what was just an appeal, a stimulus for the party, done improvised, took on poetic and political contours (Lindolfo Filho, 2004: 137).

The growing precariousness of the living conditions of the popu-lation immersed in musical entertainment became a political move-ment, so that "*reggae* gives birth to rap" (Lindolfo Filho, 2004: 135). The references to an array of African origins continuously hybrid-ize, thereby sustaining Black cultural production in the world. For Herschman (2000), when, in Jamaica, Kool Herc and Grandmaster Flash used electronic music techniques, such as *sound systems*, mix-tures of sounds and electronic rapping, "they were sustaining the emergence of rap" (p. 19), which later, in the 1970s, would change the course of Black culture in the US.

In the search for clues to the origins of *hip-hop*, it is worth noting that, in addition to Jamaica and the United States, the historical trajectories, especially those of rap, are associated with traditional cultural practices from Africa which people are re-creating today — in which oral language plays a central role. On special occasions, the griots (men) or griottes (women), chroniclers, publicly oralize mem-ories, stories of customs and deeds of societies, taking responsibility for disseminating teachings through the word, and were considered a source of culture and knowledge. Masters of the art of storytelling, they are educators, storytellers, artists, poets and musicians, whose role in the community is to recreate and disseminate ancestral cus-toms and memories[29] in everyday life.

Lindolfo Filho (2004) gives *rappers* the title of griots of the third millennium, evidently considering the transformations and tech-

---

29   Souza et. al. (2005) state that African people brought to Brazil knowledge and technology of agriculture, metallurgy, fishing and also celebration rituals, ways of using languages and the custom of telling stories as a means of forming and informing people, of reviving, rescuing, maintaining, trans-forming, in short, integrating past, present and future. In Brazil, in general, the Black woman stands out as the guardian of memory: she is the one who tells stories to encourage sleep, to educate and to advise.

nological advances available to them. In their narratives, they thematize everyday life, advise, denounce, teach, taking as references aspects of the social, political, economic and cultural environment in which they live. The author points out that oral narrative, one of the foundations of rap, is the heritage of the Africans who, enslaved and scattered throughout the world, sustained their lives by recreating, producing and appropriating the musicality of new places. In the United States, religious music, for example, is recreated in *spirituals* and in gospel (the musicalization of biblical passages). These and other modalities blend together and are transformed and reinvented from generation to generation.

To think about African cultural matrices, permanence and changes in *hip-hop*, I borrow the words of Hall (2003), for whom the fundamental is "not what traditions do to us, but what we do to our traditions" (p. 44). This argument is important not only for considering the emergence of *hip-hop*, but also for thinking about the continuous transformations that *hip-hop* undergoes, taking into account the clashes of these political and cultural processes.

To understand how this cultural configuration known as *hip-hop* became known in the world and acquired different contours, New York is still the main reference. It was there that, between the late 1960s and early 1970s, an important period for the history of African Americans, marked by the intensification of struggles for civil rights amidst protests, physical confrontations, rallies and boycotts, Blacks organized themselves to change segregationist laws. The strong racism and the explicit manifestations of prejudice and racial discrimination fed the agenda of demands for the formulation of public policies capable of responding to the specific needs of the North American Black population: changes in unfavorable laws; access to public goods, services and equipment; and better working conditions, among others.

Important activist leaders, such as Martin Luther King, Angela Davis, Malcolm X, Rosa Parks and others, became references for other organizations that emerged at the time, such as the Black Panthers, whose goal was to create a Black state capable of changing the association of forces that until then had favored only whites. The hallmark of society was the creation of separate places for Blacks and whites through the sedimentation of ideas of inferiority naturalized by socio-economic inequalities.

Later, the *Black Power* movement emerged, with a relevant role for the dissemination of a political vision based on Black African references that launched the slogan *Black is Beautiful*, exalting attitudes and gestures that could raise self-respect and *pride in being Black*. The ideas that started circulating in the USA gained expression in musical culture,[30] in clothing aesthetics and especially in hair[31] — colored, frizzy, raised, curled — showing how intentions circulated, and still circulate, crossing borders and gaining re-creations related to local cultures.

As far as the economy is concerned, American society underwent an extreme crisis: the process of deindustrialization, and the rise of unemployment. Besides this, there were changes in the role of the State that were reflected, for example, in the weakening of welfare or income transfer programs. At that time, Americans were also grappling with the Vietnam War, which contributed to the dramatic picture, even more so for part of the population — mostly Black or Hispanic — sent to the combat fields and who suffered from the consequences of maiming, death and physical and psychological debilitation.

The picture described served as a backdrop for the first expressions of *hip-hop*, embryos of a culture that would later make sense in the trajectory of part of New York's Black youth. The political and social scenario meant the intensification of restrictions and economic deprivation felt in the daily life of the ghettos.

As some studies note (Dayrell, 2005; Herschmann, 2000; Andrade, 1996), the Bronx, a Black and Hispanic neighborhood, is the privileged locus of the emergence of *hip-hop* culture. With the fraying and limited reach of social programs, young people increasingly occupied the street, resignifying it as "the place" to spend their lives, play basketball, date, listen to music, dance, sing and learn. The street

---

30   Like other Black musical genres, soul was born in the church around 1970 and has as its great icon the singer and dancer James Brown, who passed away in 2006. One of his greatest hits was "Say it out loud: I'm Black and Proud!

31   Hair is one of the central aspects in relation to the phenotypic and identity traits of Black people (Gomes, 2006).

also brought the need for the creation of leadership, which also implied being a place of debates and involvement, on different scales, with theft and drug trafficking, which generated harmful consequences, or even the death of members of groups or gangs,[32] mostly for males, a segment on which the impossibilities of inclusion in school or in the world of work fall more heavily.

As a space for sociability, it is in the street itself that community initiatives began to emerge, aimed at fostering more actions of solidarity in a universe where exposure to violence and rivalries was the main issue. These initiatives were understood as survival strategies undertaken so that a whole young generation would not be exterminated by the physical and symbolic violence represented by the lack of perspective within the social framework.

In this environment, musical culture took on new dimensions, and the increase in activities related to the arts was considered as an alternative for bringing young people together. Singing and dancing came to be seen as a way of giving another meaning to urban and youth practices. Several studies credit Afrika Bambaataa, an activist who saw the use of the sung word as a means of resistance and survival, with being one of the first to glimpse the contours of what is now known as *hip-hop*. Considered the "pope of rap," he coined the term *hip-hop*[33] in mid-1978 by combining the arts of MC, DJ, dancer and graffiti artist. The Jamaican experience influenced him and served as a basis for organizing large parties and meetings between young people, where rivalry shifted from physical confrontation to confrontation on an artistic level. At these parties, it was important to cultivate the challenge anchored in the idea that competition, in which the dexterity of the body takes center stage, was the purpose of the gathering.

Another response to the Black tradition was *rap*, which emerged in the black ghettos of New York City during this pe-

---

32   According to Abramovay et al. (1999), the word gang can be used to designate a youth organization, or a group of young people, sometimes linked to recreational activities, but generally associated with acts of delinquency and transgression.

33   Afrika Bambaataa is one of the founders of Zulu Nation, an organization that, focusing on racial discussions, has become one of the largest in the global hip-hop cultural movement. Also present in Brazil, Zulu Nation is a worldwide organization that defends knowledge and the production of knowledge as pillars of the hip-hop universe. It is considered the fifth element, along with the others — break, graffiti, MC and DJ.

riod. Grand Master Flash [a DJ] developed scratching — creating sounds by manually spinning the record under the needle in reverse — and backspin — extracting a rhythmic phrase from the record, repeating it several times, and changing the normal tempo of the song — turning vinyl into a real musical instrument and making the disc jockey, or DJ, a central figure in rap. At street parties, which increasingly attracted young people, DJs lent their microphones so that young people could improvise speech to the rhythm of the music. They were the masters of ceremonies (MCs) (Dayrell, 2005: 46).

The new forms of competition were extended to the use of the word, the ability to create rhymes that accompanied the beat, and the rhythm orchestrated by the DJs. Maintaining the word and "delivering the message" required a commitment to perfecting the techniques of composing the lyrics, maintaining the rhythm of the dance and animating those present at the parties. The MC, the master of ceremonies, was born. In the neighborhoods, the people formed groups with the aim of innovating in order to leave their mark on the environment. The sound, the dance, the rhymes, the messages, the look were key elements to appear and stand out in the scene.

The emergence of such values impregnated speech and attitudes, contributing to the creation of codes and orientations that were validated in the groups that came together, gaining strength and skills to show at parties. Once formed, these groups, bound to a certain neighborhood, joined those from other neighborhoods, creating the crews, collectives baptized with names that expressed their new identities under construction. As a substitute for gangs, collectives allowed for the practice of closer social interactions and the negotiation of interests that became common in *hip-hop* culture.

Hip-hop culture is by itself heterogeneous since, like other manifestations, it is created and remade in a hybrid way, especially in large capital cities.

It is the cosmopolitan vernacular exchanges that allow the popular musical traditions of the 'First' and the 'Third' World to fertilize each other, and which have built a symbolic space where the so-called advanced electronic technology meets the so-called primitive rhythms (Hall, 2003: 38).

Given the contours that the phenomenon assumes, another statement by Hall (2003) is very important at a moment when, also in Brazil, *hip-hop*, as well as samba and other Black cultural productions, is not infrequently understood "simply in a nostalgic and exotic notion of recovering old rhythms" (Hall, 2003: 38). This view makes it difficult to understand musicality as part of diasporic history, and thus as a way of doing politics and maintaining the literacies of reexistence.

THE URBAN CONTEXT OF SÃO PAULO: DIALOGUES WITH HIP-HOP

It is fundamentally important to situate the emergence of *hip-hop* in Brazil, which occurred within a very unique socio-political context. Between the end of the 1970s and the beginning of the 1980s, after the decline of almost twenty years of military dictatorship, the unions and civic movements took over the streets. The hyperinflation phase, the increase in the unemployment rate and the precariousness of living conditions fostered demonstrations by entities and organizations that, through collective actions, sought to influence the consolidation of the ongoing political transition: they wanted their voices to be heard and their demands met. One of the evident aspects of the period is the intensification of social inequalities, along with the increase in the strength of political parties and unions.

Added to this is the strong presence of social groups and movements that can be understood as "collective attempts to promote a common interest or secure a common goal through action outside the sphere of established institutions" (Giddens, 2005: 357). In this sense,

> The novelty that broke out in 1978 was first enunciated in the form of images, narratives, and analyses referring to the most diverse civic groups that erupted on the public scene claiming their rights, starting with the first one, the right to claim rights. (Sader, 1998: 26).

With "something new emerging in the country's social history" (Sader, 1988: 26), various segments of society, such as women, Black people and mothers, faced with their dissatisfactions and specific needs, sought to organize themselves in collective actions, later named new social movements — NSM — and showed forms of participation in, and appreciation for, cultural practices, politicizing everyday life and showing significant mobilization capacity to influence laws and public policies (Sader, 1988; Gohn, 2002; Andrews, 1998).

Brazil was experiencing the effects of a fall in employment, which affected different sectors of the population, but especially those in urban areas. The period is also marked by important strikes that expressed political, economic, cultural and ideological characteristics. In her study on the period of the bank workers' strike in 1985, Blass (1992, 178) highlights two existing perspectives of the confrontation: that of pressure and that of the mode of expression. Characterized by the party which, according to her, influenced union practices in the following years, the "festive" ways of presenting claims to the State and employers are relevant, as is establishing relationships with the population and the media. This claim for rights in the form of a "party" contributed to giving visibility to urban spaces in cities, such as the old center of São Paulo.

The old center — comprising the triangle formed by Praça da Sé, Vale do Anhangabaú, Praça da República and adjacent streets — concentrated a significant part of the banking sector, services and public institutions which, incidentally, always employed a large contingent of the Black population. It was, and still is, a corridor of intense street commerce, employment agencies and bank branches. Besides being surrounded by all means of public transportation, it stimulates the flow of people from all regions of the city, as Altair Gonçalves, or Thaíde, one of the founders of the Brazilian *hip-hop* movement, reveals when telling César Alves (2005) about his approach to this culture:

> [...] me and a friend, who is until today one of my great street brothers, Mário - who founded with me the Back Spin b-boy group -, went out to look for a job in Center Norte. The mall was still being built and they said that jobs were opening up.

We went there to see if we could find something. When we arrived, they informed us that there were no more vacancies. So, returning home, we decided to go downtown. At that time, there was still no information about breaking, except what was on television. But we already knew that there was already such a dance on 24 de Maio Street. When we got to the place, there was an agglomeration, a hell of an uproar, a large gathering of people, where a sound was playing. [...] We spent the afternoon watching the guys. That hit us hard (p. 26).

It is in this scenario that, around 1980, in São Paulo and Rio de Janeiro, a dance and a type of music emerged that would later become part of the *hip-hop* culture, still without being characterized as a sociocultural movement, and without glimpsing the reach and influence it would have in the following decades. Many activists of the *hip-hop* cultural movement, when evoking their memories, cite that when they sought employment and participated in these moments of sociability, they were, without knowing it, on a path of approximation with *hip-hop*. Memories show the city as a scenario centered on survival, in which the search for inclusion in the labor market, the need for leisure, sociability and cultural circulation made the Black population take the center of São Paulo as a reference.

By reoccupying a place and appropriating ritualized symbols, the movement reinvented traditions, defined by Hobsbawm and Ranger (2002) as:

> [...] a set of practices normally regulated by tacitly or openly accepted rules; such practices of a ritual or a symbolic nature aim to inculcate certain values and norms of behavior (p. 9).

By imprinting its style and aesthetics on the center of the city of São Paulo, *hip-hop* places itself in memory in a way that establishes temporary ties of solidarity that, collectively sustained, were fundamental for guaranteeing the survival of captive or liberated Blacks during the time of Colonial Brazil.

In the process of occupying the city, the actions of people, Black groups, Candomblé houses and associations linked to the Catholic religion, such as the Black brotherhoods, stand out. Among them is the Nossa Senhora do Rosário Sisterhood, located in Largo do Paissandu, which, especially during the 19th century, was a space for assistance and resistance, becoming a reference for the organization of enslaved or freed people.

> For Black people, the brotherhoods and sisterhoods represented the possibility of saving their humanity and living the hope of better days. In this sense, the essential functions of these associations were to protect, rescue and help their members in times of difficulty and illness (Cezerilo, 2002: 33).

The sisterhoods/brotherhoods, even after the post-abolition period, remain in an oscillating and conflicting movement between the sacred and secular dimensions, also carrying the tension of balancing the acceptance of guardianship and the search for autonomy in relation to the ecclesiastics.

In the following periods, other organizations in the city took shape, which sought to face the dictates imposed by the industrialization process, which prioritized the urbanization policies of capital. The new political, economic and cultural configurations forced the transformation of a set of activities, with a view to sustaining the ways of occupying urban spaces, mainly concerning housing, work and, in particular, forms of sociability and different Black cultural practices, which were out of tune with the project of modern society and the yearnings for progress intended for Brazil.

In different ways, Black people, and also white people in a similar situation of precariousness, sought, on the outskirts of the city, alternatives to the expulsion processes which not only allocated them to places far from the urban center, but also restricted the possibilities to access the goods and services that began to appear in the city. The street, which used to be a space for sociability, also began to be denied.

Against the impediments "to the people of color" in attending social clubs, especially in the city of São Paulo, at least two entities appeared in the 1960s aimed at the Black population: the Aristocrata Clube, more frequented by liberal professionals, self-employed or civil servants, and Clube 220, aimed at workers and employees in commerce and industry. Both, says Félix (2006), promoted leisure activities, social gatherings and balls as a reaction to racial segregation and also to encourage discussions and debates on issues that focused on "finding" Black people's place in Brazilian society. It is interesting to point out that the person responsible for the "music" at the balls was a figure very similar to what we now call a DJ. He was the one who "commanded" the record on the turntable, thus setting the tone of the parties.

To celebrate "being Black," Club 220 organized, among other activities, the "Bonequinha do Café" (Coffee Doll) contest, which crowned the most beautiful Black woman in São Paulo on May 13. The event, held in the Igreja da Irmandade dos Homens Pretos [Church of the Brotherhood of Black Men], took place in a public space from 1962 to 1977, the year in which some Black organizations present at the party held a banner with the slogan "Stop racism in Brazil!" This moment was followed by the reading of a manifesto criticizing the discrimination and racial prejudice experienced by Afro-Brazilians. The event marked the history of the Brazilian anti-racist struggle.

The 1970s created a favorable climate for the growth of Black political mobilization in favor of emancipation. Reflections of the social and racial barriers still experienced by Black people were felt, and there was a more direct questioning of the legitimacy of these parties as a space of struggle and resistance.

At the same time, references were made to Black movements abroad, which occurred together with the process of political opening and the occupation of the streets of capitals by social movements.

At the same time, in 1978, two events help to compose a picture of the heightened racial tensions: the death of a young Black man by the police, and also the expulsion of four young Blacks from the traditional Clube de Regatas Tietê, frequented by wealthier white people. The events won space in the press and, in April and May of that year, became the trigger for the political focus to be more explicit and addressed by the groups that aimed to pressure the government as well as the authorities for actions to combat racism and discrimination (Andrews, 1998; MNU, 1988).

At that time, the *Movimento Negro Unificado* [Unified Black Movement] — MNU — was founded in a public act that took place on the steps of the Municipal Theater in São Paulo, when a Charter of Principles, with signatures from representatives from several states, was read in the presence of more than 500 Black representatives. It was:

> (...) of a concentration of black people protesting against racism in a country where military dictators propagandized the existence of racial democracy. This public act of July 7th, 1978 also marked the birth of an embryonic a Black movement at the national level (Andrews 1991, 123).

Also in the 1980s, against the emergence of social struggles, evidenced by the mobilizations of workers in São Paulo and metallurgists in the ABC region,[34] the center of São Paulo was often consumed by public demonstrations organized by different entities — activists of the movement organized by women, young students, Blacks and professionals from the banking, health and education sectors, among others. According to Sader (1988), it was a moment when new figures entered the scene, challenging the existing institutional mechanisms and establishing new values and attitudes in the political field.

Moreover, for the Black social movement, the first half of 1980 was marked by the intensification of criticism against racism through acts that denounced, reclaimed and proposed actions in favor of the Black population. A series of meetings took place at union headquarters, church halls and in the academic centers of some universities, usually in the evening or on weekends, invariably accompanied by readings and discussions that could serve as ways to understand the condition of class and race in Brazil. In the meetings, written materials began to proliferate, many still mimeographed, circulating from hand to hand: bulletins, newsletters, book reviews and poetry by Black authors. Some activists not only engaged in the MNU, but

---

34   T.N.: The ABC region, also known as the ABCD region or simply ABC, is a metropolitan area located in the state of São Paulo, Brazil. The name "ABC" is an acronym that stands for the first letter of each of its constituent cities: Santo André, São Bernardo do Campo, São Caetano do Sul and Diadema. These four cities are part of the Greater São Paulo metropolitan area and are located in close proximity to the city of São Paulo itself. The region is an important industrial and economic hub in Brazil, known for its manufacturing and automotive industries.

also in political parties, especially the *Partido dos Trabalhadores* — PT [Workers' Party], something new and promising in the political environment of that time.

It is noteworthy that large galleries were located in the surroundings of the 24 de Maio Street, with dozens of clothing stores, hairdressers and products, records and electronic equipment, all important items to produce the parties that, since the 1970s, were held with greater intensity on weekends, both in clubs and in the halls of the center and in distant neighborhoods. In these spaces and environments, there was a concentration of people who were either involved in the promotion and sale of tickets, or who wanted to know the news and information relevant to the musical universe in question. It was there that the fashion for Black youth was dictated: what to wear, how to dress, how to talk, where to go and what to listen to; how to dance to soul, samba-rock and then funk. There was a strong identification among the people who attended through the symbols and values shared on the street and at the dances.

> In the spaces mostly frequented by Black people, we also observe the search for a social existence distanced from racial discrimination, lived daily in the streets, in society. At the *black* balls, for example, they exercise their self-esteem and more: their condition as citizens (Malachias, 1996: 10).

For people, the power of identification made it common to leave work and "stop by the gallery" before going home or to school, or even to come from the most distant neighborhoods of São Paulo to the center, just and exclusively to meet with their peers and to organize entertainment, to talk, *to see and be seen*. In addition, it was possible to enjoy services that they could only find in these "Black places," like clothing and shoe stores or hair salons.

Chic Show, Zimbabwe, Black Mad and *Company Soul* are the names of groups, linked to the universe of *soul* or *funk*, that professionally organized dance parties. Their members had records, national and imported, they rented halls and had the structure necessary to produce dance events. Part of these groups became professionalized and continue, to this day, to entertain in halls and clubs, as places that serve young people and those who are over 40 years old. It is not rare in these parties for two or three generations of people to dance together in the same physical space (Malachias, 1996; Félix, 2000; Macedo, 2004).

Some of those involved in Black social movements frequented the universe of Black music, but there was no direct or explicit relationship between the two. On the contrary, to some militants, the regulars of the "gallery" were party people and less politically engaged. These so-called "party people," in turn, claimed that the militants only talked about politics and were averse to parties. In this scenario, *hip-hop* culture was accepted: it emerged and developed, taking on significant dimensions and helping to make explicit the integral relationship between party and politics, between culture and social movements. *Hip-hop* arrived on the scene at a time when intellectuals, both inside and outside the academic sphere, were developing research and important studies in which they came to understand that, for the Black population, politics makes and is made by culture. Festivals and cultural production produce effects in the communities where they take place, displacing social roles and location, creating a sense of belonging, politicizing everyday life, and creating networks that allow the appropriation of new knowledge and ways of acting.

The branding of *hip-hop* as street culture reveals that, besides being characterized as a mode of artistic intervention, the movement enacts a way of living and expressing oneself, in which public places were used as spaces for social and cultural practices. In the street, the order was to occupy the spaces to dance, have fun, create and compete.

Dancing favored the creation of groups, which called themselves *break* teams, to develop and rehearse the marked steps of choreographies that, collectively, create and sustain the notion of belonging to a community.[35] The quality of participation was marked by dexterity in dancing competitions called battles, which measured the potential of group members, revealed new talents and gave respect and power to those who stood out.

---

35   Here it is interesting to note that the formation of dance teams is similar to what happened in funk and soul dances. It is yet another intertwining of the diasporic thread present in Black culture.

In the streets, in addition to the break groups that have been expanding, gaining expression and visibility, there are MCs from *rap* groups, DJs and graffiti artists. It consolidates the confluence of the four artistic languages that, to this day, sustain what is called *hip-hop* culture or the *hip-hop* cultural movement. These languages are materialized in four figures: the MC, the DJ, the dancer and the graffiti artist.

MC

At a *hip-hop* event, the master of ceremonies, MC, conveys the message, recites and sings poetry, usually that he or she has authored. His or her role is to use the voice to talk about everyday life; he or she, through poetry, highlights aspects of the social and cultural context and shows how they relate to global and local issues.

Image 2: MC Sharylaine on stage. Photo by Tiely Santos

Each MC delivers his sung word in a style that makes him stand out from the rest. We cannot forget that the dimension of "competition" is always present. Generally, it occurs in what activists call *free style*, improvised speech in the form of verses, over the beats of the DJ, concerning subjects, events or themes. Here it is possible to perceive a similarity with *repente* — a musical style typical of the Northeast region of Brazil. In the absence of a DJ (you can't always count on a stereo) or to simply show off your skills, there are other variations, such as, for example, the *beat box*, a technique of producing beat sounds and musical equipment with your mouth. The MC himself, or someone accompanying him, can use this technique to set the "tone" of the *rap*.

DJ

The art of being a disc jockey, DJ, is to elaborate sound compositions that, in record players and/or computers, showcase the techniques that bring together diverse sounds and excerpts of other songs, combined and reassembled. The function, through the handling of the equipment, is to create and sustain the cadence in the *hip-hop* environment, party or presentation.

The styles are varied, and each DJ leaves his signature on the DJing, either when he is accompanying an MC, or when he is leading a party by himself.

Image 3: DJ at the turntables performing during the Hip-Hop Week at Ação Educativa in 2000.

B-BOY OR B-GIRL

The uniqueness of each dancer contributes to the montage of this scene with their loose and colorful clothing. Dress is the ideological framework that seeks to affirm identities. In Black culture, art, musicality and physicality are ways of creating and maintaining sociability, something fundamental for everyday existence.

The dancer can use a variety of styles to get his message across, from a mechanization of the body expressed in broken movements, arms and elbows that mimic robots, to spins and acrobatics that show unique agility.

Those who dance use body language to express themselves. It is important to show this responsive body that speaks and interacts not only with the other elements of *hip-hop* culture, but also with what is happening around it. The performances show flexibility, agility and dexterity with techniques created and recreated by b-boys and b-girls.

Image 4: Hip-hop dancer Nara Ramires. Photo by Evandro Lima Silva.

GRAFFITI

Graffiti is a multi-semiotic text that blends the verbal and non-verbal, using different techniques and styles to intentionally disrupt the urban landscape. The graffiti artist paints significant themes about the moment in which we live. Classically, works that expropriate walls and facades are used to "send their message."

Until graffiti was recognized as art, many artists were beaten and arrested as "troublemakers," but even though their writings were restricted, they continued to find ways to maintain their subversive art. Today, some graffiti artists, mostly white and middle-class, exhibit their work in galleries or are invited to paint in public spaces. It is also interesting to observe how schools, through workshops or art classes, in an attempt to involve students and the community, have embraced graffiti as a valid and relevant artistic expression. This does not mean that these artists have overcome all the challenges, as many cannot express their art in a socially legitimate way due to the cost of production — spray-paint, supports, rolls and brushes.

Image 5: Tiago Vaz's graffiti art

HIP-HOP AND THE INSTITUTIONS

Another aspect that marks the trajectory of *hip-hop*, with greater emphasis after 1990, is the more explicit incorporation of the signs of struggle and resistance related to aesthetics and festivity in its forms of expression. If before this period it was a matter of occupying the street spaces to dance, have fun, create and compete, now it was a matter of understanding and acting against the police repression and accusations of disturbing public order.

With this in mind, the groups began to operate in closed spaces such as NGOs, schools and community centers. Being closer to their places of residence, they began to be more aware of everyday problems such as violence, police repression and unemployment. In order to understand why these areas had such problems, they began to meet more systematically to discuss, debate and present solutions to daily confrontations. Participating in activities such as winter clothing drives, fundraising parties and speaking at schools and community centers, allowed for an exchange between *hip-hop* culture and everyday life in the *periferia*.

In this context, the need arose to create an entity that represented the different groups that were scattered across the regions of São Paulo. According to Andrade (1996), the configurations of *hip-hop* culture were now being redefined. The MH20 — *Movimento Hip-Hop Organizado* [Organized *Hip-Hop Movement*]— was created in 1989. This second phase was marked by an interest in knowing the references already incorporated into the universe of demands made by African Americans, such as issues related to civil rights, in the *hip-hop* movement in the United States.

> In the early 1990s, we found the influence of the second generation of North American *rap* among São Paulo *rappers*. At that moment, the struggle for the civil rights of the black population and the mobilization of internationalized Afro-American symbols were integrated into the discursive universe of groups such as *Public Enemy, NWA, KRS One, Eric B* and *Rakim*, among others. References to Africa, Malcolm X, Martin Luther King, Black Panthers, Islam are present in songs, video

clips and album covers. These symbols also became familiar to São Paulo *rappers* (Silva, 1999: 29).

In the face of social and racial issues, new directions and goals began to emerge. The meetings began to be attended by members of organizations linked to the Black social movement, who saw these youth organizations as a productive space for the development of highly visible activities so that their discourse could reach and be meaningful to a greater number of people. At the time, Geledés, a political organization focused on women's and youth rights and working against racial and gender discrimination, supported the Rappers Project, responding to a demand from groups of young people who were victims of police repression. Between 1992 and 1998, the Projeto Rappers developed several strategies of visibility and support, including the publication of the magazine *Pode Crê!*, focused on *hip-hop* culture, and served as a reference for projects in different parts of Brazil, including governmental ones.

In São Paulo, the intensification of these exchanges leads to the awareness that street culture is more than dancing, more than rhyming: it is also a space for contestation in the face of racism, racial discrimination and social inequalities; in this context, "*rappers* emphasize that 'self-knowledge' is strategic in terms of understanding the trajectory of the Black population in America and Brazil" (Silva, 1999: 29). Due to this aspect, there has been a greater investment in the search for support and qualification for speech, which intensified the *rappers'* contact with sources and spaces that signify the possession of knowledge, which is almost seen as a condition for action, as Silva (1999) points out.

With the density of new information, *rap* shifts from a style characterized by fast speech and lyrics with content that is less critical of social or racial issues — chatty *rap* — to a politicized style that is less about dancing and having fun and more about listening, reflecting and politicizing.

> The condition of being excluded appears in *rapper* discourse as an object of reflection and denunciation; once again (...) *rappers* speak as voices of that silenced universe in which personal and collective dramas develop in a dramatic way. Slaughter,

police violence, racism, misery, and the social disintegration of the 1990s are recurrent themes in *rap* poetics. They reflect the deindustrialization of the metropolis and the urban segregation that divided the city into fortified condominiums and poor neighborhoods (Silva, 1999: 31).

This retrospective of the *hip-hop* cultural movement offers hope for thinking about why it is so widespread in its occupation and transformation of the spaces it reaches, and also why it is now recognized as a cultural and political movement for developing socio-educational practices, resistance and self-affirmation. In a way, *hip-hop* is affiliated with a notion of education, in a broad sense, as explained by Silva (2003) when dealing with a conception of education based on an African model.

> Only those who use education to progress in becoming a person, which implies being part of a community, are educated. The community, a territory of coexistence, is formed and maintained in the set of relationships among people that allow each one to exercise, develop, and enrich his energies, potentialities, and knowledge (p. 186).

In these models, education would be important for people to learn to "lead their own lives" (Silva, 2003), benefiting collectively from learning, as happens in other cultural expressions of the Black diaspora: *capoeira, maracatus, jongo, maculelê, candomblé terreiros, congadas, sambas, batuques*, soul and funk circles, in which the different forms of participation have made sense and represent, for the Black population, opportunities for exchange and sociability in the educational process of several generations.

THE PRACTICED SPACES OF LITERACIES

In the *hip-hop* universe, one of the central issues is the need to produce new ways of experiencing and appropriating socially constructed knowledge; in this sense, the use of language becomes fundamental. The groups have sought ways to make visible the new ways of relating to cultural practices whose centrality lies in written, gestural, pictorial and musical language. Participating in *hip-hop* has meant learning to enter the literate universe, changing the naturalized images of the literate practices of young people from the *periferias*, the Black and poor young people.

In the most diverse activities that young people carry out, the use and movement of diverse props are present — biographies of historical figures; music lyrics; history books and videos — materials that come from different sources: borrowed from libraries, donated, lent to the groups. One of the functions of activists involved in *hip-hop* culture is to disseminate values that have served as a reference for sustaining literacy practices capable of responding to their demands and interests, as well as those of the community in which they live.

The appropriation of meaningful knowledge brings participants closer to the lives of African descendants, not only in Brazil but also in the United States, while also addressing issues of class and, more recently, gender inequalities. Although the appropriation of knowledge can take place in a diffuse way, amid various activities such as concerts, debates and lectures, some groups still value meetings as a privileged site for the circulation and production of knowledge. Such meetings, which may or may not take place in the neighborhood itself, require planning: choice of location (usually a given space); negotiation and request of the location; scheduling of dates and times; calling of members; organization of the site. In the meetings, the items on the agenda are discussed; there is also the distribution of tasks, the development of the meeting with or without a written record and the combination of new meetings.

In general, the actions developed collectively also include the discussion of issues related to the structural living conditions of the community, or even proposals for local improvement, such as campaigns and solidarity actions, and claims against the government, which are configured in new uses of written and oral language.

Not infrequently, it is through participation in non-school spaces that the use of written language is valued, as it acquires meaning in everyday life.

Although the activists validate school knowledge and see the school as an important agency, we can affirm that if the process of literacy is guided by different social institutions, and agencies with different dynamics and characteristics, we can consider the *hip-hop* movement as a space of practices that, without being fixed or sufficiently institutionalized, generates possibilities for using language in literate practices.

In this universe, in the various practices of language use that are mobilized in communities, activists act as literacy agents whose characteristic is to:

> Know the means, weaknesses, and strengths of the group members and their local practices, mobilizing their knowledge and experience, their "ways of doing" (including the use of leaders within the group) to carry out the targeted activities: getting around, locating, collecting, playing, researching (Kleiman, 2006b: 11).

Often without the means for their work, they show themselves as agents, creating alternative conditions and training others through their experiences, in which they bring into focus the notions of learning and teaching of what I call literacies of reexistence. In these practiced spaces, a multiplicity of processes emerges that, in relation to the most diverse contexts, involve both socially valued and under-valued uses of language that refer to shared and, above all, reinvented intentions and goals.

> Here lies the opacity of "popular" culture the black stone that resists assimilation. What is called wisdom there is defined as a trampoline, a word that, in a play on words, is associated with the acrobatics of the acrobats and their art of jumping on the trampoline, and as trickery, cunning, and cleverness in the way of using or circumventing the terms of social contracts. (De Certeau, 1994: 79)

From the *rap* lyrics to the experiences they idealize and provide, activists emerge as individuals who resist dogmatic language that establishes only one "right" way of using language, the standard, and who seek to legitimize and take possession of other ways of entering the literate world. Again, these are characteristics of a literacy agent, an actor who, even without many available resources, mobilizes "tactics, resources, strategies, knowledge, and the availability of technologies" (Kleiman, 2006b).

In the literacy events carried out by activists, the word is invested and given specific contours that combine aspects such as the socio-historical context of production, the goals of the speakers involved, the intertwined power relations, the dynamics and the multiple ways in which language is used socially.

In order to understand the complexity of these literacy practices, in the following chapters I will identify, within speech, the singularities of these practices and the action of *hip-hop* as a literacy agent. Furthermore, I will seek to know the positioning of the subjects as agents of literacies that move in non- school socio-cultural contexts that seem to redefine their social identities.

CHAPTER 4

MOVEMENTS, AGENCY AND EMERGENT AGENTS

I don't just read books because I don't believe in books. That is because I know that, somehow, an author wrote it. I don't know who that author is, /.../ a person, even though they research about something, they have their own ideas, and I don't believe in books very much (.) that's why, like, I do read, I like reading, (.) but /.../ then: I listen to people, sometimes I go — I have been to a terreiro.[36] I have researched with people who have been playing for a long time, and then I (.) like, here they talk a lot about the griots, you know, (.) historians. They would come to the villages and tell stories.
(Débora)

I t is necessary to understand how the activists who are part of the *hip-hop* culture appropriate and produce unique practices of social language use.

During the first *roda de conversa*, the research participants were surprised by what they had discovered about each other's reading practices: what they read, how they read and what they got from the various printed materials they had access to, such as books, newspa-

---

36   T.N.: In Candomblé, a *terreiro* is a sacred place where religious ceremonies and rituals are performed. Candomblé is an Afro-Brazilian religion with roots in the Yoruba, Fon and Bantu cultures of West and Central Africa. *Terreiros* are central to the practice of Candomblé and serve as the religious community's gathering place.

pers, pamphlets or advertising materials for cultural events. In the group, the discussion about the importance of exchanging impressions, beyond the stages or meetings to organize activities, gained more substance when they presented the collections they shared in their homes.

This moment of exchange was an excellent opportunity to propose to the young participants the development of a narrative in which they would be able to reconstruct for others the stages of their lives that they considered significant.

In this context, the young people would write for the participants in the discussion groups and read their productions to others in the following meeting. As preparation, we talked briefly about how we could generally consider the main stages of human life — childhood, adolescence and youth — and within each stage, relationships with family, school, peer group, social participation and work. Without a rigid timeframe, they would choose what to say, organize the moments and decide how to narrate.

The narratives[37] are not the focus of this chapter. However, along with the interactions and individual interviews, they form one of the tips of data triangulation. In order to conceptualize the narrative, I will consider Bruner's (1995) assumptions, according to which the subject, when narrating, puts his or her memory into action to evoke and select some events of his or her own life.

The narrative can be understood as a product that contains different and complementary stories. It becomes an enumeration of events, like a chronology, in which one highlights the remarkable events of one's life, i.e. when one goes to school for the first time and when one gets a job, among other important moments. They give meaning to some of the events, thus creating chronicles in which experiences are detailed. To give an example, starting school, as happened to the young participants in this research, can be attributed to the experience of racism, among other aspects of our society. The elements present in the chronicles are interwoven into deeper stories:

---

37   In the design of the research project, narrative was considered as one of the tools to generate data.

The process of 'organizing an autobiography' is a skillful act of transferring a sampling of episodic memories to a dense matrix of organized and culturally schematized semantic memory (Bruner, 1995: 147)

As they brought their own interpretations of the significant events in their lives to the narratives, the research participants made visible the chain of discourses on which they rely to shape their identities. Although they were unstable and limited to single episodes, they also revealed the literacy practices they developed at different moments in their lives.

SELF-NARRATIVES: LITERACY JOURNEYS

Dimenor

"Biographing poetry"   Dimenor — The unknown biography

How can I have a biography if my childhood was stolen? Memories come to me in full force when I lie down.

I remember the little boy in his childhood who, instead of flying kites, ran like a blast to pick up bottles and cans.

Come back home happy with some coins and some blood coming out of my nose cursing everyone you miserable! I provided the bread for my 2 little brothers! 7 years living this life, school, cans, feet hurt by screws and glasses, but still happy because I could buy milk to feed my brothers.

There goes the boy from Itaquaquecetuba, born in the late 70s, in Suzano.

Understanding, reason or illusion, at the age of 8 Ipiranga, São Paulo became my new city, prejudices that haunt the Angolan descendants who learn about their history in the real school, "life."

Prejudice and discrimination became my worst enemies, a hidden shelter when they be looking at this nigga expecting me to always be a failure and be living a fucked up life and that the capitalist media would try to narrow my mind, but then I saw a light at the end of the tunnel, I mean inside the tunnel, São Bento, subway hip-hop, status an era with no fame only the best outfits on, white vultures in black, setting fire to the real Black rooted culture.

What a pity!

Maybe not! However, after 15 years I can say that I really found what I was looking for.

At 25, I can raise my hands to the sky and thank my orishas and ancestors for allowing me to live to this day so that I could find what I've always been looking for, even if I didn't know what it was!!!

"My Autobiography"

Although it was a small achievement, it was a big step in proving that Black people are valuable, recovering our memory and realizing that Black people are not only made up of sadness and suffering.

We are also made up of love, joy and assertiveness; I know that we are the majority of the population.

Dimenor getting out of here

Still looking for an answer

This is my logic for sure

No matter how long it takes

Won't make me sad

It makes me happy

Cause I know what I think and what I say

A *favelado*[38] man

Proud to be

Black!!!

Axé!!!

LGE

(…)

When I was 5 years old, I started school in Itaquera. I wasn't a bad student, despite the problems I had to face at home and in my daily life, like my father's alcoholism; although my mother was a strong woman, she couldn't stand the fact that my father always came home drunk. We moved to my grandmother's house, which was in a middle-class neighborhood in São Paulo. It was hard for me to adjust to my new school "friends," a bunch of wannabe rich kids, and I am the kind of boy who does not take bullshit. I didn't isolate myself from everyone, but I didn't really open up to people. In school I had three best friends, they were my brother, my cousin and our neighbor. I had "acquaintances" at school. I was sad because my mother used to work and I had to be away from her all day. I also missed my father, who only visited us on weekends.

(…)

Time passed and we managed to accomplish our things. I started working when I was young and I hardly saw my family because my mother worked a lot. I became an adolescent and continued to work and study, although it was a very turbulent period. Despite the fact that I was always at home, I started going out to clubs. I did everything from good to bad. I was still quarrelsome, but never at home, because I was very nice to my family.

I learned about *rap* when I was fifteen or sixteen years old; at first, I just wanted to know about women, alcohol and drugs. But then

---

38   T.N.: *Favelado* is a term in Brazilian Portuguese to refer to someone who lives in a slum (*favela*). The term used to be pejorative and has been resignified to empower slum dwellers and highlight their positive contributions and achievements.

some time passed and I started to learn more about the racial issues in *rap*, demanding better conditions for the people and claiming the rights of citizens, especially those of African descent. When I started composing, I could not stop. I identified with a brother named C.D.P. He was my friend who encouraged me to read books. At first, I didn't like it very much, but I started to like reading with time. Before that, I read because I had to, not because I liked it.

(/..../[39])

During my recovery, I got involved with NGOs and institutions, I started teaching rhyming and giving lessons on the self-esteem of Black people.

/.../

I became more passionate about my life, rapping and helping those in need through education and civic awareness.

I am currently working with the youth and participating in the youth movement. Always with the help of *rap* and my mother who has always been by my side in good and bad moments.

Soneca

In my thirties, I suffered, I had fun, I was disappointed and I had a lot of fun. My life has always been intertwined with this city, where I have always lived in different parts of the South Zone.

I had a good childhood, despite the fact that I was discriminated against for not having the same financial status as some idiots. I had many allies, a square, the street, 2 rocks on each side of the improvised football field. Many games were possible in this way and they happened. /.../

That's how I grew up, with many allies by my side. Today, many of them have gone astray, and the result is that some have been arrested and others have died.

---

39   /.../ indicates that the researcher removed an excerpt. The participant narrates that he loses his job; his father dies; he gets married and then divorced; gets involved with alcohol and drugs; gets sick; seeks help to recover.

/.../

Well, when it comes to my school life, it was terrible. It wasn't easy for my mother, poor thing.

I had to endure many suspensions, written warnings and even compulsory school attendance. All of this was because I was rebelling against the school because I was being discriminated against. I didn't mind not having the best clothes because I knew my family did what they could. I never really cared about clothes, but when my friends and I were being discriminated against because of the color of our skin and the way we dressed, we got together to scare off those who looked down on people at school. They had nice clothes and money, but attitude and personality are things you cannot wear or buy. They are things that come with you and sometimes you get them by going through hard moments in life.

Well, my school days weren't that bad. Up to the 6th grade I had never failed, but then I met other rejected kids in Group C of the Zerbini V. Arapuá School. It was in this group that, after many fights and suspensions, I was transferred to another school in the process of forced enrollment. /.../

From that moment on, the school I was attending asked me to leave. I failed the sixth grade many times but in different schools. Then, 10 years later, I returned to the supplementary school where I passed the year, stopped, passed again, and stopped again until I graduated from the supplementary school in June 2004.

That's how I spent my adolescence, troubled at school and fooling around on the streets. I was targeted, and with my allies by my side, I endured many stop-and-frisks. Sometimes four a day, the cops followed us. It only got better when Diadema's complaint [against the police] became a known fact in the Naval *favela*. From then on, it happened less often. ((In the excerpt removed, Soneca writes that he left home, lived on pensions and endured many deprivations)).

I saw the face of death a dozen times in those days. Many clubs, drugs, alcohol, women, nights where hunger and misery walked side by side with my allies and the wrong path...

Well, nowadays I have a *rap* group called *"Lado Obscuro"* [Dark Side] — (missed part) — where I talk about discrimination, what it makes people do and the situation. Because of everything I've lived, I feel it's my duty to help my own and those I haven't met yet, but I know they're in a hard situation.

Together with *Posse Senzala Urbana* and now with the group formed by our warrior "Analu," I have developed projects to promote and create activities related to *hip-hop* around communities in need. I've been doing this for 7 years and I'm not even thinking about stopping. I don't know if I will make money with my *rap* or my activism, what I know is that my reward is: "To recover!"

Débora

Roda de conversa[40]

I started going out when I was 11, but always with my cousins. So, you know, there was always somebody taking care of me. And all that time I wouldn't say no to a fight, and whenever I went out I would pick a fight with somebody. Those fights got me into really difficult situations /.../ That's why I like to say that I don't take shit from anybody. It was the same at school. They used to call me a gang leader in my school because sometimes I would get outraged when the teacher said something and then I would fight with the teacher. People sometimes want to look down on you /.../ but they forget that we also have knowledge that doesn't come from school. My father studied a lot. He even started university, and even though he didn't finish it, he can teach me a lot of things about rights and so on. And the teachers, well, okay, we have to respect them, but they have to respect us too. Some of them think we're ignorant about some things, but it's not really like that.

/.../ well, my reactions were always like that /.../ if I think something is not right, I will show myself how it is... I think it's my right to say my opinion and to fight. If something is right, I will stop and listen, but... In the same way that I was aggressive, I was also a very good friend to people. Those who needed me reached out to me.

---

40   Débora read her biography to the group. I didn't use transcription conventions to make it easier to read.

When I got involved in social projects, everything changed a lot, even my critical view. Maybe I'm not very charismatic, but through the projects, I learned a lot of things I never learned at school. /.../

Then, still in the project, I learned about music, and it was something that I fell in love with...well, I realized that I've actually liked *hip-hop* for a long time, I just didn't know the name /.../ they prepared me really well in the beginning, and then I started working with production, but nothing with much evidence. I met a lot of interesting people during the culture week, it was very nice because you see people who look kind of rough /.../ people who are really in need, but who are nice people.

And that was pretty normal, you know. Everybody was talking, so somehow I started to accept myself even more. There was also the issue of race. I always saw my father struggling. He watches movies and writes letters to, I don't know, newspapers and stuff like that. He has a lot of anger in him, sometimes I try to understand and since I was very little I started to understand and I also started to live as a different person /.../ When I entered a project where most of the people were Black, so you know how it is to feel at home? No matter how bad the project is, you feel good. That was the moment when I started to be around Black people of the same social status as me. You know what I mean? I started hanging out with people that I felt good with and going to parties that were thrown out of the blue. Like barbecues, birthday parties /.../ That's how we did it, and meeting people, you know, it was very nice. /.../ *hip-hop* /.../ it was many years ago, like three years ago, and my self-acceptance came because of that...you know, seeing myself and fighting for things, then you start to understand and accept yourself, fight for what is diverse. And you also show people how cool it is.

Nathas[41]

Individual interview

/.../ Magazines were all I had to read at home, my mother used to bring them from the place where she worked at Arno's support

---

41   Nathas's text is part of an individual interview.

center. They had cocktails and things like that, and my mom would bring the magazines and we would flip through the pages. The textbooks were the same and focused on the content of many subjects.

/.../ I liked to read medical leaflets from a very young age, it was because I used to take care of my little sister, right, my parents had to work and I liked to read the medicine to know what it was for. I liked to read; I still like to read. I always read the leaflet first when I have to take medicine.

My mother always worked hard, my mother always worked very hard. Even though my dad lived with us, my mom was the one who always took care of me and my sister, so if I'm someone like... I don't know, with more awareness and responsibility, it's because of my mom.

I went to pre-school when I was about 2 years old. I stayed there until I was 6, almost 7, so I left pre-school and went straight to elementary school. Everything was normal until my 5th grade year when I went to school like everyone else. After 5th grade, I started skipping school to play soccer and video games. Then I failed 5th grade. And I also failed the 6th and 8th grades because I was always absent and also because the school was very far away /.../

When I was in high school, I only went to 10th grade for a week because it was a little far away. So I said no, I'm not going back. I was out of school for a year, then I got into a school near where I lived, then I graduated. Straight, without failing. I was already into *hip-hop*.

I started in *hip-hop* at the end of middle school, in 7th and 8th grade /.../ But in the beginning, I used to have electronic music parties. There was a DJ whose brother was always with me when I was in school, bro. When I first got to the school, I thought it was one of those schools that rich kids attended, right, because it was on Paulista, but when I got there, I saw that it was completely different. People wore nice sneakers and clothes. The guys were kind of mischievous, some even said they were from a gang from Bela Vista. And I was like, oh fuck! I remember going there wearing nice sneakers that my mom gave me that day. I kind of hid them so the guys wouldn't take them off, and then he warned me. /.../

His brother was a DJ and he had all the equipment at home, the pickups and everything, but he was playing electronic music, dance music, house music at that time, stuff like that. We used to go to pubs or have parties at school. But I got into *hip-hop* after that, when I was already at the other school I went to, which was in my neighborhood. I think I was about to finish 7th grade when I started getting into it. In 8th grade, I met a guy who had just gotten out of the correctional school. He liked rap. Oh my! We got together. Like, me, my hunger and his willingness to make it happen. That's when I really got into *hip-hop*.

***

In several moments of the narratives, we can glimpse that the "lessons" that the young people learned in school are not limited to content and subjects, but extend to the problems they experienced in the school environment. Issues such as their relationship with their peers:

> It was hard for me to adjust to my new school "friends," a bunch of rich kids. I had "acquaintances" at school.

> I had to endure many suspensions, written warnings and even compulsory school attendance. All of this was because I was rebelling against the school because I was being discriminated against. I didn't mind not having the best clothes.

And with teachers and principals:

> From that moment on, the school I was attending asked me to leave. I failed the sixth grade many times but in different schools. Then, 10 years later, I returned to the supplementary school where I passed the year, stopped, passed again and stopped again until I graduated from the supplementary school in June 2004.

> They used to call me a gang leader in my school because sometimes I would get outraged when the teacher said something and then I would fight with the teacher /.../ And the teachers,

well, okay, we have to respect them, but they have to respect us too. Some of them think we're ignorant about some things, but it's not really like that.

Or even issues like physical access to transportation and school transfers to distant neighborhoods:

> Then I failed 5th grade. And I also failed the 6th and 8th grades because I was always absent and also because the school was very far away /.../ When I was in high school, I only went to 10th grade for a week because it was a little far away. So I said no, I'm not going back.

The narratives illustrate that much of what is remarkable about these young people's school lives is often what we leave aside when we think about the curriculum: sociability, peer interaction and social identity. It is interesting to emphasize that the place of interpersonal relationships in school institutions, with teachers and administrators, was more relevant than issues related to behavior or content. The value they place on school as a place of belonging explains its importance for these young people, as well as for the *hip-hop* movement in São Paulo. It is not the "school" itself that is being questioned, but what we choose to emphasize in education, how we relate to each other within it and what we can do with what we learn. The school is a space where multiple and heterogeneous literacies circulate, in addition to the multiple cultures embedded in the life histories of the most diverse individuals who access it. (Rojo, 2009; Bunzen, 2009; Vóvio, 2007; Kleiman, 2006a).

Many of the literacy practices valued by the activists took place outside the school environment, without this implying an aversion to schooling or the value it may have.

Entering the *hip-hop* universe is a pivotal moment for the activists, taking on an almost salvific sense of giving their lives a purpose: usually the purpose of "saving" them from a life of violence, without dreams and goals, or building their self-esteem. It is thought-provoking to note the transformative power of *hip-hop*: it is given so much importance in the narratives that it ends up being as important as family. Highlighting the role of the family becomes fundamental, especially the mother figures, in encouraging them to respond and build other possibilities for themselves that are less destructive and more positive.

The following excerpts show how each of them interweaves their narratives with memories of their experiences with their families, in school and within the *hip-hop* movement.

Dimenor: racial issue – hip-hop and family

> I provided the bread for my 2 little brothers! 7 years living this life, school, cans, feet hurt by screws and glasses, but still happy because I could buy milk to feed my brothers. /.../ Prejudice and discrimination became my worst enemies, a hidden shelter when they be looking at this nigga expecting me to always be a failure and be living a fucked up life /.../ but then I saw a light at the end of the tunnel, I mean inside the tunnel, São Bento, subway hip-hop, status an era with no fame only the best outfits on, white vultures in black, setting fire to the real Black rooted culture. /.../ However, after 15 years I can say that I really found what I was looking for.

LGe (Leandro): language use, hip-hop and family

> I learned about rap when I was fifteen or sixteen years old; /.../ But then some time passed and I started to learn more about the racial issues in rap, demanding better conditions for the people /.../ When I started composing, I could not stop. I identified with a brother named C.D.P. He was my friend who encouraged me to read books. At first, I didn't like it very much, but I started to like reading with time. Before that, I read because I had to, not because I liked it. /.../ I am currently working with the youth and participating in the youth movement. Always with the help of rap and my mother who has always been by my side in good and bad moments.

Soneca: school life, family hip-hop and his commitment as an educator

Well, when it comes to my school life, it was terrible. It wasn't easy for my mother, poor thing. /.../ I didn't mind not having the best clothes because I knew my family did what they could. /.../ Well, nowadays I have a *rap* group called "*Lado Obscuro*" [Dark Side] — (missed part) — where I talk about discrimination, what it makes people do and the situation. Because of everything I've lived, I feel it's my duty to help my own and those I haven't met yet, but I know they're in a hard situation.

Nathas: reading, discovery of hip-hop in school and family

Magazines were all I had to read at home, my mother used to bring them from the place where she worked /.../ I liked to read medical leaflets from a very young age, it was because I used to take care of my little sister. /.../ My mother always worked hard, my mother always worked very hard. Even though my dad lived with us, my mom was the one who always took care of me and my sister /.../ I started in *hip-hop* at the end of middle school, in 7th and 8th grade /.../ But in the beginning, I used to have electronic music parties. There was a DJ whose brother was always with me when I was in school, bro. /.../ But I got into *hip-hop* after that, when I was already at the other school I went to, which was in my neighborhood. I think I was about to finish 7th grade when I started getting into it. In 8th grade, I met a guy who had just gotten out of the correctional school. He liked rap. Oh my! We got together. Like, me, my hunger and his willingness to make it happen. That's when I really got into *hip-hop*.

Débora: identity, hip-hop and family

My father studied a lot. He even started university, and even though he didn't finish it, he can teach me a lot of things about rights and so on. /../ Then I got involved in social projects, everything changed a lot, even my critical view.

/.../ but through the projects, I learned a lot of things I never learned at school.

/.../ I realized that I've actually liked *hip-hop* for a long time, I just didn't know the name /.../ they prepared me really well in the beginning, and then I started working with production /.../ Everybody was talking, so somehow I started to accept myself even more. There was also the issue of race. I always saw my father struggling, he watches movies and writes letters /.../ He has a lot of anger in him /.../ *hip-hop* /—.../ it was many years ago, like three years ago, and my self-acceptance came because of that...you know, seeing myself and fighting for things, then you start to understand and accept yourself, fight for what is diverse. And you also show people how cool it is.

Through the narratives of the young people who co-authored this book, we learn that they not only face adversity but also have a political commitment that they see as a result of their involvement in the *hip-hop* movement. It is not that *hip-hop* is the only important element in their lives, but it is also a significant commitment that has led to questions about the different ways the collectivity finds to re-exist and to connect with different reading practices. This has given space to the networks they have built to transform themselves into heterogeneous networks, to give some meaning to their choices and to mark the similarities and differences they have with certain groups, thus constituting their social identities.

The narratives, together with an analysis of discussions in the first *roda de conversa*, helped me to identify the dual role that reading plays in the lives of these young people: one function is related to their experiences in the school environment and in their daily lives, and the other is related to less institutionalized spaces created to appropriate certain writing practices, such as those developed in *hip-hop* and street collectives. What I call school function and life function are not closed categories that don't talk to each other. Rather, their school experience, though sometimes unpleasant and disruptive, has its importance recognized in the student's journey, as do experiences in other educational settings, such as the family, the street and peer groups.

I have yet to show how the relationship, the space in-between, the third space (Bhabha, 1996), the place where I am simultaneously close and distant, will point to the materials they produce.

GIVING MEANINGS TO THE READING COLLECTIONS

Considering that my goal is to identify the literacy practices in the activists' narratives, as well as the value they give to the experiences they have had in the universe of *hip-hop*, I bring some excerpts from the first *roda de conversa*, in August 2004, right after the meeting where they filled out the surveys. They gave us important elements that allowed us to understand the movements and circumstances that give meaning to their expressions.

During the *roda de conversa*, after the initial greetings as we gathered around a table,[42] Nathas responded to my opening greeting for the event (Matencio, 2001) in a provocative and teasing way:

1. Analu: Hello, folks, let's go?
2. Nathas: Who hasn't done the homework?

Nathas's question evokes a common literacy event in the school environment; the teacher is usually responsible for moderating the discussions, whose role in the interaction authorizes the control and command of the students' actions. In this moment, Nathas assumes the role of the person who can demand from all his classmates an action they agreed to, which is to bring the reading materials, or homework as he calls it. In doing so, he modifies the framework of power relations, creating the typical asymmetry that sustains the relationship between teacher and student in the school universe and that will also sustain the research situation in the *rodas de conversa*. He tries to give me, the "outsider" researcher, through words that act ideologically, a different place than the one responsible for conducting the interaction.

If, on the one hand, he acts discursively and creates another ritual marked by subversion, taking a position and placing the other participants as a group that can be demanded, on the other hand he

---

42   Nathas, Soneca, Débora, Dimenor, LGe and I were in the first circle. The meeting was held at night and took about two hours.

establishes a dialogue and responds to the classical event of academic research, which involves a game marked by asymmetry between those who research and produce knowledge and those who are most often the objects of the research.

This is just the beginning of the conversation, the result of a reasonable negotiation period during which the activists insisted that the meetings be part of a process that would allow for the formation of other positions in relation to the roles typically occupied by researchers and the objects of research.

Nathas's initial statement functioned in the process of data generation as the tip of an enunciative thread that, in the course of subsequent meetings, in the midst of "poaching operations" (De Certeau, 1994), was cunningly woven into the elaboration of a resistant and revealing fabric of socio-cultural practices and singular positions of language use.

I take over the word in response to Nathas's statement, amplified by the laughter of the other participants:

3. Analu: No, come on, so the idea is (.) not necessarily about who did or didn't bring, but to spea:::k about what you like to rea:::d,(.) about what moti:::vates you, stuff like that, come on::

My response sought to establish a relationship of complicity and collectivity in order to subsequently mitigate the charge of Nathas's speech: *It's not necessarily about who did or didn't bring it*, and finally, in explaining the action to be performed by the participants: *but to spea:::k about what you like to rea:::d, (.) about what moti:::vates you, stuff like that, come on//* in order to then assume the role of someone who leads the *roda de conversa* and, therefore, the research.

In the sequence, in response, some of the group members began to place on the table several materials that they understood to be their reading collections. We can evaluate the action as an expressive response (Bakhtin/Voloshinov 1995 [1929]), both in relation to Nathas's statement and to mine. The following photograph, linked to the context of data generation, illustrates the categorical way in which they responded to the provocation:

Image 6 — Reading collection. © Analu

Considering that studies of situated literacy practices also attach importance to texts and cultural artifacts that are part of everyday life, it is worth briefly analyzing photography as a witness to reality (Hamilton, 2000: 16-33) by marking the visual characteristics of the group's collections. It is a diverse collection that includes newspapers, magazines, books and discursive genres, usually legitimized by people with some social engagement or seeking information on social, political and economic issues, race, rights and current affairs.

The materials on the table functioned as a motto to express the place and role of written language in the concrete situation of interaction in the *roda de conversa*.

4. LGe: Oh, I'm quite eclectic

5. Analu: Go deeper then…

6. LGe: I think I /…/ I like to read a bit of everything, from nove:::ls to comic bo:::oks (.) I (.) prefer reading to watching TV, I think information is better located in reading, (.) so (.) what I brought,

some literatu:::re, (.) some newspape:::r// (pointing to some of the material on the table).

LGe supports his image of an eclectic reader who reads what he likes. In an argumentative scale marked by the operators *from* and *to*, he explains that his collection includes readings that are considered more socially prestigious, such as novels and newspapers, as well as readings that are neglected by the school canon, which generally describes these readings in a derogatory way, as minor. Comic books are an example of such a practice. By positioning himself as an eclectic reader who reads a little of everything, he shows autonomy from the hierarchies that assign different values to certain readings. Then, instead of continuing to describe his reading preferences, he decides to say that he prefers reading to watching television. He gives importance to reading when it comes to being informed, which he says is his focus. He also takes a positive stance on current discourses that denounce the decline of reading habits and point to the growing audience for certain television programs as the main cause. His quest for information makes him an eclectic reader, which means that he reads different things in order to be informed.

The *rapper's* preference for materials that feed him with information is similar to one of the principles of *hip-hop*, which is anchored in the valorization of information, seen as raw material to process the chronicles of everyday life. The informational function of reading is crucial to uncover a part of history that has not been told, to enter spaces where we can appropriate the knowledge that has been denied or restricted, to organize knowledge and to put the word out into the world, whether written or not, in a mindful and therefore careful way.

LGe was one of the participants who brought the most reading materials, which made the other group members tease him: "He didn't bring more because his suitcase was being washed," and he replied:

14 LGe: The funny thing is that's true, (.) so, I gotta read a little bit of everything, I read *Carta Capita:::l⁴³/* to see what's going::: (.) on, and even so sometimes folks will say, (.) *Contigo⁴⁴* bro, will you read *Contigo?* We gotta read *Contigo,* you gotta see the information, like::: Playboy Magazine, as people say, brings lots of information, I've never bought a Playboy to get information, let alone to see naked women/.

In his speech, the *rapper* shows the others that he has "done his homework" by citing magazines and describing the value and importance of the publications to him. First, he appreciates *Carta Capital,* which is aimed at a middle-class adult audience. The magazine covers business, politics and culture and is considered "good reading."

He also appreciates *Contigo,* which covers news about actors, actresses and TV show hosts, the celebrity world, soap operas and music. It is classified as a women's magazine. LGe, by incorporating *hip-hop* voices into his speech with the vocal impositions and intonational contours typical of quoted speech — *But you, bro, a rapper, a man, are you going to read Contigo?* —, trying to respond to an ideological word of someone who may judge this kind of reading as a futile, banal, amusing and perhaps uninformative.

Finally, he takes a step in the direction of expanding the group of "valid informative readings" by declaring that he will not buy or read Playboy magazine, which, according to him, is good for others but not for himself: *Playboy Magazine, as people say, brings lots of information, I've never bought a Playboy to get information, let alone to see naked women.* Despite marking the position of someone who owns his knowledge, his choices are close to discursive genres that are already established and without necessarily being contested. His discourse seems to be related to the socially legitimized perspectives to categorize what is interesting to read and what is not.

---

43   T.N.: *Carta Capital* is a Brazilian weekly magazine published by Editora Basset Ltda. It was founded in August 1994 by the Italian-Brazilian journalist Mino Carta. It covers a wide range of topics, including politics, economics, culture and society. It is known for its progressive and left-leaning editorial stance and often provides analysis and commentary from a progressive perspective.
44   T.N.: *Contigo!* is a Brazilian entertainment and celebrity magazine. It covers a wide range of topics related to celebrities, popular culture, entertainment, fashion and lifestyle. Between 1963 and 2018, it was a very popular magazine in Brazil.

He chooses the word information to carefully show that his eclecticism is motivated by the need for self-education and by a commitment that responds to a duty: I have to read a little bit of everything, thus showing that the search for information is something valuable and requires evaluation and that he's able to assign different weights to different reading materials.

Following the *roda de conversa*, I invite Nathas to continue:

20 Analu: Cool, (.) and you, Jonata?

21 Nathas: Well, me too, (.) I like to read a bit of everything, a little bit of everything, whatever is within my reach to read I will read, but (.) when laziness doesn't take over, right? ((laughter)) (.) Sometimes we are lazy to read, get a book, o:::h my. (.) and to read it, later (.) I don't have time to rea:::d, then I read you know whe:::n (.) then I forget the initial discussion, then I gotta retur:::n to it, you know? Now more /.../ because whenever I am able to (.) what is short (.) I will be reading, if it's short, if it's long, a thick book, for instance (.) that I need to read and then (.) it lacks time (.) then I stop reading, o:::h I will stop here, I come back to it in a while, (.) then time passes and passes

The expression *me too*, in Nathas's statement, evokes aspects of LGe's statement, thus creating an alliance with his partner. In expressing *I like to read a bit of everything, a little bit of everything*, he is in chorus with his friend who preceded him. He would also be an eclectic reader, if we consider that he reads a little bit of everything and reads whatever is within his reach, adding to the singularities present in the argument that laziness, lack of time and difficulty concentrating make it hard for him to read.

When he decides to talk about the book as an object of reading, he seems to establish a dialogue with the social voice that gives the book the status of a valued and legitimate object. On the other hand, he also creates tension and questioning by bringing up laziness and lack of time as important aspects of reading: *Sometimes we are lazy to read, to get a book, o:::h my. (.) and to read it, later.*

We can see in the statement a movement away from reading when he attributes his difficulty to laziness. When he uses the pronoun "we" — *sometimes we are lazy to read* — he includes other people in the status of "lazy reader," a similar opinion to that of other young people who claim that they don't read because they are lazy. However, it is necessary to point out that the lack of time seems to be a much greater determinant than the lack of taste for reading. Unfavorable living conditions and the struggle for survival often make it impossible to immerse oneself in reading. Laziness here can also be understood as "exhaustion" due to the daily struggle.

The next excerpt presents another way of relating to reading. The lack of time to read is still mentioned as a justification for selectivity. Soneca's speech emphasizes the social functions of reading: to inform and to mobilize emotions.

24 Analu: Check it out (.) is this your reading?

25 Soneca: yeah. It is (.) this is my reading, because I don't (.) I don't read very much you know? (.) then:::, (.) I've read only few books, right, one of the books I've read, I was telling you, it's *Papillon*, right? (.) I fell in love with the history because it was a::: (.) guy who— he was trying /.../ He had his own way to make a living, right? Robbing banks, you know? They couldn't catch him in a way, they killed a homeless person and::: blamed it on him, right? Then::: his capture was very suffering, he (.) was trying to escape from prison. I fell in love with the story of the book, get it? I think— I think, he ran away he was betrayed, he went back to jail, (.) then he believed in a nun (.) in the middle— in the middle of the story of the book he believes in a nun (.) understand? (.) a priest and they say they will accommodate him, but they betray him again. The movie portrays pretty well what human beings are like

Soneca's statement: *yeah. It is (.) this is my reading* shows his solidary orientation with LGe and Nathas's statements. In the sequence, he describes and qualifies the way he reads: *because I don't (.) I don't read very much you know?* By speaking of a "done on the go" reading, that is, done in the middle of many other daily tasks, he shows that, for him, literate social practices are embedded in the activities he takes part in.

The fleeting readings, performed according to the needs arising from different situations in broader social contexts, are valued. Reading that allows one to act in diverse and complex situations is revealed as an activity embedded in daily practices, something central in the *hip-hop* universe: it is not about reading for reading's sake but reading for a reason and with a purpose. This reading embedded in the daily routine is in contrast to a reading that requires time, silence and appropriate space to stop and read, which has to do with concentration and the possession of a determined and silent space.

If activists had to rely on socially authorized places to relate to reading, perhaps such a relationship would not exist. They invent ways of reading in mobile and unstable spaces that depend on the actions of the subject to be established. It is not a matter of establishing a place associated with an ordered activity or with the inert, "and making a grave of it" (De Certeau, 1994: 201). What these subjects construct is a heterogeneous, noisy, mobile space of literacy practices that "therefore has neither the univocity nor the stability of a 'proper' space (ibid.: 202)." As agents, makers and inventors of "practiced spaces," it is in the street, a privileged site for their practices and sociability, that they subvert a static relationship to reading, showing that "everyday life is invented with a thousand ways of unauthorized poaching operations" (ibid.: 201-207).

When developing the theme, *the book I liked to read*, Soneca does it uniquely, by attributing meaning to a reading that had an effect and value for him. When he chooses to say that he *fell in love* to describe the relationship he built with the story — *I've read only a few books, right, one of the books I've read, I was telling you, it's Papillon, right? (.) I fell in love with the history* — he indicates his affectionate relationship with *Papillon* and helps the audience understand why he chose to talk about that specific one and not another object. In his statement, the valuation and appreciation for the material he read reveal the meanings surrounding his reading practice. It is noticeable that he remembers the character's rough life story and portrays him as a resistant person, capable of making alliances, even when he is deceived and betrayed. Papillon is a fighter, despite the fact he had faced so many unfavorable and unfair situations.

The activist's analysis resonates with his experience of appropriating the contradictions of human relations and social issues that strongly affect those who live on the margins. It is impossible not to draw a bridge between his life's journey and the daily struggle in the invisible yet tangible war for survival and self-affirmation. Soneca's statement humanizes the book, which ceases to be an object, a thing, and instead comes to life in the communicative context.

Influencing people seems to be Soneca's intention, as he asked more than once during his speech if the audience understood what he meant. It is possible to get a glimpse of his success in the statements of the group participants as the interaction continues:

> 39 LGe: I think you identified with the book (.) with the reality you live, (.) or am I wrong?
>
> 40 Dimenor: Oh, me too, I think there is some sort of inspiration too.
>
> 41 Soneca: Yeah::: (.) more or less, right, bro?
>
> 42 What you saw, or I dunno, something is similar//
>
> 43 Analu: How old were you when you came across that (.) *Papillon* guy?
>
> 44 Soneca: Well, I was 19 years old (.) eleven years ago, only ((laughter))
>
> 45 Analu: Oh (.) Look at him::: ((laughter)) (.) a long time, right?
>
> 46: Soneca: a long time//
>
> 47 Analu: a:::h, not that long.

Here he gives the word "reading" the value it deserves, giving it a different function, one that is no longer utilitarian or merely informative. It is associated with a function closer to affection since it involves identification with the hero of the novel. It is a more enriching way of reading for pleasure: a life lesson. During the circle, those who speak and those who listen agree on the meaning given to the plot of the book and begin to value reading more, considering that there is an encounter between the narrative and the individual who identifies with it.

In his speech, Soneca shows the affective bases that sustain his relationship with the book, establishing bonds and opening possibilities for dialogue from another place with his "bros" and "sis" and with academia, now not only as an analytical and engaged reader, but also as a reader who appropriates the text as a support for thinking about life. Knowing how to look and analyze the sources that help us understand human beings in their social, cultural, political and economic determinations is fundamental for those who act as *rappers* by singing the struggles of everyday life. The statement makes explicit the three-dimensional character of speech when it is possible to realize that:

> The speaker, the topic, and the listener appear as constitutive factors of speech, essential to its existence [...] The listener is defined as the individual the speaker takes into account, the one to whom the speech is oriented, who intrinsically determines the structure of speech (Barros and Fiorin, 1994: 21).

If, at the beginning of the conversation, the intention was to know "who did or didn't do the homework," as the conversation progressed the interest fell on the books they had brought and the reasons why they had chosen them, as we can see in LGe's question, indirectly addressed to Debora.

543 LGe: Yeah. Why did she bring *Negras raízes* (.) I wanna know.

544 Débora: It's a book I've just started reading, like::: (.) I've read this kind of book before::: /.../ there are other books that I didn't bring, there's one by Ferréz called *Manual prático do* ódio [The Practical Handbook of Hate], that's it. it's::: a different side of the history, it's the story of the i:::ndigenous peoples, tellin' their side of the history, like, what they suffered, (.) telling (.) about the Portuguese colonization. This is a book that I am still in the beginni:::ng, (.) then I stop, this is the way I read, I don't read just books because I don't believe in books. That is because I know that, somehow, an author wrote it.

I don't know who that author is, his work was translated (.) Because he's a (.) it's about the history of the United States, etc, everything starts there, he (.) I know he goes all around the world to learn Black people's history, (.) but someone wrote it (.) a person, even though they research about something, they have their own ideas, and I don't believe in books very much (.) that's why, you know, I do read, I like reading, (.) but /.../ then::: I listen to people, sometimes I go — I have been to a *terreiro*. I've::: done research with people who have been play:::ing for a long time, and then I (.) like, here they talk a lot about the griots, you know, (.) It's something I would like to find. Griots are (.) historians, they would come to the villages and tell stories, to those who don't know (..) I didn't know, I used to call griot, but it's fine, and::: (.) it was in one of the classes we had here during the *Hip-hop* Culture Week that I learned with Da::nDa:::n about stuff like that, you know, (.) we were talking. Today I will go to the Culture House where he is teaching, etc, I said. Man, I want to attend your class.

In the context of Débora's narrative, the appreciative emphasis of the object of speech changes again: the value of written culture is relativized by questioning the veracity and legitimacy of each author, since they come with a specific context and their own interests. Débora states that she distrusts the author, does research to learn more, checks if what she reads is reliable and evaluates if the material can be part of her selective repertoire. In this sequence, there is a clash with the canonical view of reading, which says that one can validate the written record as true: *I don't read only books because I don't believe in books. After all, somehow, it was an author who wrote it, I don't know who the author is.* In the position of resistance concerning the supremacy of the book, she dethrones the letters and affirms that what is not written is also a valid and legitimate source of information: *I do read, I like reading, (.) but /.../ then::: I listen to people, sometimes I go — I have been to a* terreiro. *I've::: done research with people who have been play:::ing for a long time.*

In her discourse, Débora deconstructs the object of discourse being constructed in the *roda de conversa*: the valuation of reading as a unique, universal source of knowledge. Moreover, by putting the author "under suspicion" with a discourse that disconcerts the established norm, she creates fissures in the vision of authority generally attributed to authors. She questions the power attributed to writing to legitimize some and exclude others, including the participants of the *roda de conversa*, due to their identity.

If writing has an owner, it is the reader who owns it. The reader holds the power to make writing something that can also belong to them, something that is aligned with their life. Débora claims her authority as a reader to legitimize or not legitimize a book by using other sources of knowledge, such as orality.

When she talks about her preferences, senses and beliefs, she brings ancestry and African references to the scene through the *ogans* from Candomblé, the men who are initiated in the African-Brazilian traditions and play the drums to worship the orishas and the griots.

She "reads by ear" (Chartier, 1991; Moysés, 1995). For her, reading takes place through listening, movement and verbal interaction. She uses orality to research, talk and create networks of knowledge to elaborate discourses and identities. In Débora's words, she is interested in reading that puts her in motion, which somehow represents her daily life as a young Black woman and activist. For her, the legitimate "writings" are those created by "incarnated" people with whom she can talk, share and bring knowledge impregnated with ancient forms of learning (Souza et al., 2005). Here, reading takes on a function that can be seen as a tool for challenging the established social order.

In the circle, the perspective of appropriation and re-signification of knowledge is always present, making the interactions a space of learning and identity building. Débora's words echoed, and were echoed by, the other members in a way that created a sense of strangeness because it represented an opposition to the positive position of writing that the male activists had been expressing until then. Her statement shed light on the fact that the writing they were talking about did not give voice to people who came from Black popular culture, since it excluded orality and Black diasporic representatives who were important for the political and racial education of the activists. The fragment below explains this tension and shows the male members' attempt to reclaim the word in order to maintain the spotlight that had been theirs.

> 596 Dimenor: No, because when she said she does not believe in books (.) I said it was nice that she was saying, (.) 'cuz I don't quite believe in books too (.) I read them (.) but I don't believe, and he saying that people don't have the reference (.) they search for the reference. Then when you say, here in Brazil you say, *I want to know who my African ancestors were (.) what part of Africa my ancestors came from. (.) Were they brought here or to the United States* (2.0) *and came here from there?* So /.../ it works that way, Black people (.) in Brazil, (.) o:::r let's research about the history of Brazil, you know what I mean? Everyone talks about Zumbi dos Palmares, but no one talks about Anastácia (..) Dandara, (..) Dona ehh (.) Clementina de Jesus//

> 597 LGe: João Cândido//

> 598 Dimenor: So, nobody kno:::ws, man. There are many out there, Luís Gama, no one knows who he was, they only know Zumbi, be cause Zumbi be /.../ became part of the narrative of the youth and became trendy (.) Che Guevara became trendy//

> 599 LGe: Pelé//

> 600 Dimenor: Everybody, you know, (.) everybody became trendy//

> 601 LGe: Brazil's revolutionary//

> 602 Analu: You were speaking about yourself:: /.../ that — that:: if we want to talk about history, it's not necessarily (..) in books//

> 603 Dimenor: That's it//

> 604 LGe: No, of course, because books weren't made for you to agree with them, they were made for you to be self-critical, man, (.) they were made for you to put them there/for you to discuss/you know? For you to build some sense, bro//

Dimenor makes Débora's voice his own, characterizing a dialogism both in terms of more immediate interaction with the other, and also in the fact that he establishes a dialogue with Débora's discursive positioning concerning writing and reading. In the statement *'cuz I don't quite believe in books too (.) I read them (.) but I don't believe,* what at first may seem a rejection of the importance of reading and writing illustrates the use of a socio-historical filter that acts on this reading object, according to interests, intentions, expectations, etc.

The knowledge that makes sense concerns a set of information that, for Dimenor and the other members, is validated as Black people's word, an ancestral knowledge that recovers a history of resistance overlooked by the official version. This knowledge empowers because it links the collectivity to a common historicity of Black diasporic culture. Dimenor talks about the need to take ownership of the references that have been denied to him: *I want to know who my African ancestors were /…/ let's research about the history of Brazil, you know what I mean? Everyone talks about Zumbi dos Palmares, but no one talks about Anastácia (..) Dandara, (..) Dona ehh (.) Clementina de Jesus.*

This is the speech of an educator who is concerned with retelling the story in a way that Black people appear as subjects of their own narrative and history, thus giving new meanings to the experiences of being Black. He cites historical characters that, in one way or another, are important to delineate the tactics Black people have used to make their stories continue reverberating in their moveable identities (Hall, 2003), despite the silencing and struggling with multiple social voices documented in the interlocutors' speech.

In the *roda de conversa*, it is possible to notice that the core collections are those that help the participants come up with answers for themselves as *rappers*. What is the place of orality? What is worth reading? How do the readings circulate? In the following excerpt, one of the questions refers to the search for self-recognition in the books they have read.

39 Soneca: I was 19 years old (.) and::: (.) despite the fact I liked— I liked (.) the book very much, I read it several times because (.) I found myself discriminated against// in the book (.) in the book the guy suffers a lot of discrimination, so I relied on the book, right? at the time, I ((unintelligible)) everything.

40 Nathas: And, when did you feel like (.) feel like reading?

41 Soneca: To be honest, bro, I never had the desire to read (.) this is the truth (.) understand? (.) the desire to::: read I acquired through culture, ((referring to his insertion in the *hip-hop* culture)) to get informed about what happe:::ns (.) zine, you know? and::: as a way to get things off my chest I used to read/ talk about the (.) is::: /.../ how can I put it, bro? (.) This book is the following, bro, the (.) the guy is in jail, the guy is in jail and wants to escape, I mean, even when someone is free, they are politically imprisoned (.) they also want to escape from the things that happen out there, so they feel imprisoned too.

By expressing *the desire to::: read I acquired through culture* and when referring to the search for information and the practice of reading fanzines, the participant brings into the circle an aspect of the discourses that constitute *hip-hop* culture: the stimulation to read. *Hip-hop* is thus configured as an agency of literacies that allows subjects to discover written supports, in addition to legitimizing uses that are not always recognized because they are not authorized in the highly hierarchical society we live in. In the fragments, they problematize the common saying that "young people don't read," especially when they live in peripheral regions. When Soneca speaks of a reading practice that results from a moment he has lived, a life situation — being discriminated against, like the character — he acts in an interactional perspective, uniting the character *Papillon*'s experiences with his experiences as a reader. In doing so, he maintains his appreciative horizon in relation to the reading that helped him to understand himself as also an oppressed person, a person who struggles and seeks "freedom."

The function of reading in the constitution of social identity is clear here, which also occurs in the interaction of the second *roda de conversa*: which social voices do the statements establish a dialogue with? Which ones do they reject? Which ones are legitimated? What are the effects that these approaches produce in the interaction? The interaction with the voice of the other is what provides the construction of our positions, our identities and our social voices:

In the creative relationship with language, there are no words without voice, nobody's words. In every word there are sometimes infinitely distant, anonymous, almost impersonal (...) almost imperceptible voices, and close voices, which sound concomitantly (Bakhtin, 2003: 330).

It is important to note that, in this process, the subject is not deprived of his voice and, thus, his identity, but that we can only constitute ourselves if the idea of otherness is present. Otherness is constitutive of our identity, and that is why our voices are impregnated by the other, by what the other says, by the word of the other in a relationship of approximation, distance, tension and conflict. In this sense, it is relevant to note in the analyzed fragments that the activists do not position themselves against school knowledge or against the school or the readings that circulate in it but question the fact that there seems to be only "the" authorized reading that does not always contemplate the traces of memory and history of those who come "from the margins."

MAKING LITERACY AGENTS – IN PROCESS

From the speech of the *rappers* involved in the research, we can learn how they constitute themselves as literacy agents, establishing *hip-hop* culture as an emergent agency of literacies. In order to examine the ongoing constitution of identity throughout the research process, I will examine materials and literacy events that are a part of the everyday lives of the activists interviewed. Both materials and events reveal facets of the activists' relationship to reading, writing, orality, paper and new technologies, and allow us to emphasize that language and social practice are not dissociated in *hip-hop*. I will focus my analyses on fanzines and rap, practices in which the research subjects were involved. Later, I will also analyze the cover of a CD produced during the formation of the group *Hip-Hop Educando*, as explained in the methodology chapter.

FANZINE – GENRES OF KNOWLEDGE SOCIALIZATION

Fanzines, like rap, are good material examples of the moment in which young participants constitute themselves as literacy agents. At one point in the conversation, LGe pulls some copies of a fanzine out of his bag. In doing so, he empowers this specific written production of *hip-hop* and encourages one of the group members, Dimenor, who thanks him and then takes responsibility for the creation.

> 25 LGe: I read fanzines a lot too, ((LGe takes out some copies of fanzines that were in his bag, holds them and shows them to the people in the circle))
>
> 26 Nathas: Fanzines are::: what we read most at home,
>
> 27 Soneca: I have a bunch of fanzines at home (.) too, (.) well, I (.) like to rea:::d fanzines, as he is saying here and in reality///
>
> 28 Dimenor: Thank you
>
> 29 Soneca: And::::: at the time//
>
> 30 Analu: Why did you say thank you to him?
>
> 31 Dimenor: No, because I've been making fanzines for four years,
>
> 32 Analu: A::h ok, ((laughter))
>
> 33 Soneca: His fanzine is good, advertise it,
>
> 34 Analu: And you brought a zine for us to see?
>
> 35 Soneca: Here's a bunch (.) here// ((also pointing to the material he had in the middle of his diary among other papers))
>
> 36 Dimenor: Too bad I didn't bring any.

The appreciative emphasis of the speech object is perceived in the speech of LGe — *I read fanzines a lot too* —, in Nathas's house — *Fanzines are::: what we read most at home,* — and Soneca's house — *I have a bunch of fanzines home* —, to which they attribute value for the frequency of reading and its presence in the home collection. This material is given the status of shared and legitimized reading, reflecting the reading habits of the *hip-hop* universe. As members of the movement and the new dimension it acquires, *rappers* create a discursive alliance that is relevant to the constitution of the group: a space for the formation of literacy agents who act collectively.

Collective action is not only one of the hallmarks of *hip-hop* culture, it is also an important characteristic of a social agent who is constantly seeking to expand the capacity to mobilize knowledge systems, not only in his favor but in the favor of a collective. Beyond artistic style, they establish themselves as a social action group with a political position in defense of education.

Here the notion of authorship emerges, since "fanzines" are created by an "author," but at the same time the collective character that such authorship represents is also raised. The participation of other activists in the editorial process is not uncommon, not only with suggestions but also with interventions during the creation process of the fanzine. In this sense, we can say that Dimenor, as well as other activists, takes a position closer to that of an editor than an author when it comes to making fanzines.

According to the *Houaiss Dictionary of the Portuguese Language* (2001), fanzine means magazine written by and for fans. This word comes from English, combining the words "fan" and "magazine." If we stick to this definition alone, then a fanzine is a magazine for fans of a particular cultural universe. In the *hip-hop* universe, however, the fanzine, usually consisting of one or two handmade sheets of sulfite paper, is a written material highly valued by activists that goes beyond its apparent simplicity of production and distribution. Its multimodal elaboration involves the collage of various texts — newspaper and magazine articles, song lyrics, poems and advertisements, assembly and intervention with illustrations and prints, the creation of slogans and the use of different fonts and sizes in black and white.

In the words of fanzine author/editor Dimenor, this discursive genre has a peculiar history of being in the social scene. It is worth highlighting its connection and reason for existence within "peripheral" movements.

> Dimenor: /.../. I think that people found a form of education in zines, a form of culture// a form of the alternative press because through a fanzine you could collect information, you didn't have to buy *rap* magazines, (.) through a fanzine you (.) you would get to know /.../for a guy from Itaquera to know that a *rap* magazine was released (.) a fanzine maker would have to go and say, "hey, there's such and such magazines coming out" and he would also spread the word to the big media

through the fanzine,/.../ many people that are also part of the big magazine media have already had some experience with fanzi:::nes, (.) today there are some fanzines that are magazines, /.../ today ain't (.) today there is the computer and the fanzine makers has become lazier (.) and started making fanzines through the computer (.) this is more or less the history of the /.../ a little bit of the history of fanzines.

Dimenor's speech explains the importance that the movement places on the genre. Fanzines are a point of reference among *hip-hop* activists. They are mentioned in several moments of the conversations, as in the following excerpt:

40 Nathas: And, when did you feel like (.) feel like reading like that?

41 Soneca: To be honest, bro, I never had the desire to read (.) this is the truth (.) understand? (.) the desire to::: read I acquired through culture, ((referring to his insertion in the *hip-hop* culture)) to get informed about what happe:::ns (.) zine, you know? and::: as a way to get things off my chest I used to read/

The reading materials and the meanings attributed to them refer to the characteristics of literacy agents who, without having all the structural conditions such as access to different materials, computers at home and other resources, "improvise" and struggle to forge the means of access for themselves and then for the community. What is more, by focusing on the reading possibilities they already know and validate — informative reading, fast reading, reading with images — these are the aspects that stand out when *rappers* think about the production, consumption and circulation of information, fundamental aspects for the organization of project-based work in school, which, as Kleiman (2006) and Rojo (2009) point out, are not always able to be effective. Because of their simple and cheap format, fanzines democratize and help to circulate knowledge. In this way, they promote more democratic and collective learning and help to eliminate the interdictions associated with the purchase and distribution of written materials such as newspapers and books.

RAP – ORALITY IN THE POETRY OF DAILY LIFE

The activists' practices show the ways of moving and acting through language. To highlight the movement of an assemblage of life that constitutes a situated practice of language use, I will focus on the sung word of *hip-hop*.

The same language that is often valued to disqualify young readers and lock them into a subalternized identity is transformed into a "song of resistance that denounces and uncovers the struggles and inequalities that hide beneath the established order" (De Certeau, 1994: 79), marking performances in which the body and language come together to sustain situated literacy practices marked by resistance and subversion. It happens not only because of the themes addressed but also because of the style and form that the productions take.

By listening, observing and reading the movements of language in *hip-hop*, especially in the practices of the MCs who sing rap, we can notice the appreciative emphasis announced by Bakhtin, who states that without a body there is no word. In rap, the word appears as the engine of action of the subjects who, through the language in operation, act in the world-building and constituting identities that are continuously formed and transformed, as proposed by Hall (2003).

It is worth mentioning that, in *hip-hop*, poetry and rhythm are accentuated when they together create rap. Although *rap* relates to both the rhythmic and sonic texture, on the hands of the DJ, and the lyrics vocalized by the MC, the latter stands out for being the speaker who takes the different voices in the lyrics to different spaces.

Rap is one of the genres in which we can observe the language play that sustains an autonomous, contesting, counter-hegemonic narrative, which can promote mobilizing knowledge. The sonority is so fundamentally present that even when raps are read from a written source, it is possible to "hear" them. The subversion of writing through orality gives *rap* originality and autonomy in the face of school writing that shows the inventiveness and agency of subjects who want to express the peculiarities of marginalized life through writing that is also "peripheral."

"Education is the Motto" is the title of a *rap* produced by Nathas, LGe, Soneca and Dimenor in the first semester of 2005. They presented the lyrics as a result of reflections on their inclusion in the data generation process of the doctoral dissertation and right after the collective decision to form the workgroup *Hip-Hop Educando* [Educating with hip-hop]. We will see the lyrics of the rap, then move on to the analysis, seeking to identify and recognize the meanings of the lyrics in their relationships with the ways of conceiving education in the group.

EDUCATION IS THE MOTTO

PART I

1. From Palestine to Pakistan, Haiti or Germany.
2. From Jamaica bombs Bob Marley gained much fame.
3. Mandela, Malcom X, Che Guevara and Zumbi of the military coup that took place here.
4. I open my mind and it cheats me. I have nothing to eat and no money in my pocket.
5. Pay close attention to what I have to say Hip-Hop Educando bringing some knowledge and progress.

PART II

6. Lado Obscuro in da house with Submundo Racional / Woke and bringing the real information.
7. Comin' to the scene talkin' bout school education,
8. Our folks be revolt 'cuz they ain't got no information.
9. About their culture that was not appreciated / Black history in schools is eliminated
10. Out of the classroom they be looking for information / the conclusion is seen in the library invasion.
11. Looking for books so they know the hidden truth/ due to class struggle students evade.
12. Go to the streets and get what the school won't give them/

13. Those who sit at the back of the class don't get the teacher's attention.

14. But have they wondered how much knowledge those students possess /they must provide them knowledge, leisure and education.

15. Drop out school become a criminal/ and find recovery in hip-hop.

16. It becomes a choice for the ones who be neglected/ to escape the traps that were set.

17. They might use money as bait / but intelligence is our counter-attack weapon

18. The law benefits those who own it / that's why information don't get to the hoods.

19. But the hoods be providing art education / and awareness to our sisters and brothers,

Chorus

20. Education, information is the motto,

21. Hip-Hop Educando in da house.

Part III

22. Do your thing 'cuz hip-hop strikes again,

23. My folk's information, interaction, education.

24. Spray-painted ABC, calling your attention

25. Resistance comes from us, fleeing is not an option

26. I propose a fusion and came here to rescue y'all

27. If you wanna be a B.Boy nigga you betta study hard.

28. Interact, react, be armed with knowledge

29. What they imposed on us is not always lost in time

30. Example don't only come from whiteboards, it's also in the streets,

31. Move around and get a book, go get some culture.

32. Get your respect, know your roots, become yourself.

33. Be your own way, it's better than being like them.

34. Fulfil your life with a world of poetry,

35. Riddim gives movement harmony and experience.

36. Be it in school or out there, stand up and get up 'cuz

37. Education is the key against discrimination.

38. But watch out in the streets, the world is a jungle

39. Ready to swallow if you don't go by the rules.

40. Something calls out from outside the window,

41. Get up to date, learn, cuz reading is amusing

42. Young people ain't moving they be giving in to laziness,

43. If only they got a chance, but instead they got more rules to follow

44. We do our part, it's Hip-Hop Educando,

45. Spreading hope, courage and literacy.

46. A MC and his mic feel like a call to action,

47. Submundo, Obscuro, Analu here to review the lesson.

For analysis purposes, I divided the text into 4 parts: part I — lines 1 to 5; Part II, lines 6 to 19; the chorus in lines 20 and 21; and Part III from lines 22 to the end.

In the lyrics, which introduce the newly formed work group — *Hip-Hop Educando* —, they argue that through *rap* and the meanings it produces, there is a possibility to educate, raise awareness, subvert, advise and unite. In rap, poetry has the function of "causing" an effect on those who listen. Initially, I highlight the chorus of the lyrics in lines 20 and 21 — *Education, information is the motto, Hip-Hop Educando in da house*, which, together with the title "Education is the Motto," establishes as the delineation of the group's objectives, formulated at the beginning of the research, and which is embodied during its development: to affirm the legitimacy of *hip-hop* culture.

In Part I, there is an appreciation of the pedagogical references that are important to the *hip-hop* universe and that allow activists to find ways to enter spaces of practice, spaces for constructing and validating knowledge and meaning around their identity markers. This is why they assert in line 5: *Pay close attention to what I have to say Hip-Hop Educando bringing some knowledge and progress.*

Right at the beginning of Part II, in line 6, the *rap* announces the enunciators and what the intentions and potentialities of this talk-action are: *Lado Obscuro in da house with Submundo Racional / Woke and bringing the real information.* There are two *rap* groups — "*Lado Obscuro in da house with Submundo Racional*" — that strengthen relationships during the research process. By sharing what they knew and learned, they created *Hip-Hop Educando* which constituted itself as another space for practice.

Through poetry, the speakers echo the tangle of voices unhappy with the living conditions that most of the lower-class population must face. In addition to their rights, they demand an education system that can meet the needs of all people, without discriminating and ignoring, for instance, the *students who sit at the back of the class* (lines 13 and 14), where the neglected and overlooked students usually stay.

To promote transformations in education, the agents advocate that it is not only a matter of saying what one possesses or not. It's about creating a strategy to construct alternatives that work not only as a way to speak up about the inequalities (lines 22 to 47), but also as a way to use the word to make affirmations and to put the individual and collective resistance into practice.

By narrating everyday school experiences, the *rap* positions the street as a place to learn, '*cuz they ain't got no information. About their culture that was not appreciated/ Black history in schools is eliminated/ out of the classroom they be looking for information/ the conclusion is seen in the library invasion!* (lines 8 to 12). The lyrics express that when the individuals cannot see meaning in being part of the school culture that excludes them, they go to the streets in search of something that can bring some meaning to their lives.

The lyrics establish a dialogue with data on the literacy of the Black population in the present. Even if the school does not recognize it, *hip-hop* culture is in the school, and sometimes it is not the disciplinary knowledge of the curriculum that is valued by the students, but — as we can see in the biographies of the *rappers* — the spaces of sociability that can turn the school into a space of practice where those who are part of it can legitimize what makes sense to them. As *rap* lyrics say, the street is valued as a place of information. The lyrics play the role of a wise counselor, or even griots, as Débora reminds us in the epigraph that opens this chapter when she credits the storytellers of everyday life with the important role of being a source of learning.

Part III invites people to assume their duty in the educational process: *Do your thing 'cuz hip-hop strikes again, my folk's information, interaction, education* (lines 22 and 23). *Hip-hop* appears between two spaces, the school and the street, and acquires a third space when it offers ways to counterattack: "I propose a fusion." That is, facing adversities leads us to understand that, on the one hand, *you betta study hard* (line 27), meaning that education is both a right and a duty and even though it is not ideal, *what they imposed on us is not always lost in time* (lines 26 to 29). On the other hand, different literacy possibilities can be found in the streets: *move around and get a book, go get some culture* (lines 31 to 37). The culture here does not simply refer to any culture, it is a situated culture and should promote the construction of favorable identities so that individuals can have *their own ways to exist*. It's a message from those who are already doing something: *We do our part, it's Hip-Hop Educando. Spreading hope, courage and literacy* (lines 44 and 45).

At the end of the *rap*, legitimizing and recognizing the work of the *rappers* and my own in a process of ethical research and social commitment, they say: *Submundo, Obscuro, Analu here to review the lesson.*

The expression "review the lesson" values the space of research as a place of learning, with specific academic activities, which is also indirectly valued. It is the synthesis of the collective meanings produced in the interactions as we shared, debated and reformulated knowledge and social identities.

THE DISCOURSE IN THE IMAGES

Hip-hop is multimodal because it uses different languages. This brings us to the concept that, in contemporary society, literacy practices are far beyond writing. They also involve images and visual signs (Dionisio, 2010). Having this in mind, in this section, the focus will be on the uses the group of *rappers* make of the multimodal language, and thus establish themselves as literacy agents. The aspects that establish them as such are the innovation in their social actions and the search for new resources that can convey their ideas and ideologies.

We will analyze the CD cover produced by the young participants in the second semester of 2005, when we did not meet as often as in the period from August to December 2004. The idea of producing the CD came from LGe and Dimenor, both members of the *Submundo Racional* group. After some minimal planning, Soneca was involved in the proposal: they invited other people and groups to send their music by e-mail. In order to assemble the CD, they relied on the solidarity of a friend who had a studio, since they did not fully master the technique and did not have the equipment. With the original material in hand, they joined forces to buy the media — the CDs — and counted on the editing island of a non-governmental organization to reproduce the material. In general, any work in *hip-hop* requires the configuration of a group of people from different fields. This is one of the characteristics of the *hip-hop* cultural movement and also of the young participants in the research.

Motta-Roth's reflection (2005) can help us understand the production process of the CD and its cover:

> The way we appropriate the universe and the information around us and incorporate them into our cognitive repertoire by representing, describing, and using language to make evaluations is an aspect of human beings. However, this process of appropriation is shaped by a dialogic interaction with the world (Motta-Roth, 2005: 181).

For example, when the group was discussing the theme for the CD cover, they considered Dimenor's idea of commemorating a friend who was in prison. They sketched the idea on a sheet of paper and asked an artist to finish the drawing. It took some time to digitize the artwork and turn it into a cover. At the same time, they pressed the CD. They were also responsible for presenting it at events and selling it for a symbolic price. The CD was like a calling card: "This is *Hip-Hop Educando* CD," they said. And what does the CD cover say?

We will analyze the CD cover produced by the group, considering the image as speech, to establish relationships between the verbal and non-verbal language in the text.

Image 7: Cover of the project Hip-Hop Educando / Educating with Hip Hop. Art by Bylla based on Dimenor's idea.

On the cover, the non-verbal and verbal elements play a problema-tizing role, using signs that socially represent two paths — school and prison — that are antagonistic and complementary when we give them meaning.

Although composed of different elements, the young man appears as the central figure in the drawing. The emphasis on his slightly bent body and the movement of his head seem to direct his gaze toward fulfillment and uncertainty. When the young man looks to his right, there is a demon leading to temptation and ruin. As he looks down, there are references to the fascination with illegal ways of making money (perhaps because it is hidden in a bag), luxury, and pleasures such as drinking, and the gun, associated with crime and prison, but also with power. To the young man's left is a black-skinned angel — subversively depicted in opposition to traditional white images — which can be associated with goodness, salvation, protection and school. The large books in front of the school build-ing legitimize reading and the school sphere as a place of reading and learning.

We can deepen the analysis by highlighting some aspects of the vi-sual composition, considering the image's colors, shapes, movement and positions, all of which are relevant elements to understand the discourse of the visual composition of the CD cover. Let us remem-ber that this drawing is Manichean: either one thing or another. It is a drawing for those who also must decide. There are capital letters in dark and contrasting colors, an attempt to help him make a decision. The colors are also present in the characters representing "good" and "evil."

The playful drawing of the devil has an irregular structure that suggests instability and restlessness. There is no point of balance, and the position of the hands conveys movements that indicate des-peration. The character seems to be restlessly trying to convince the boy to choose his side. The angel, on the other hand, stands on a triangular base in a position of exaltation and joy. He just watches and patiently waits for the boy's decision.

The relationship established between the two characters, part of the collective imaginary that contains Christian and symbolic moral values, sustains a discourse that promotes competition, one relying on the other to gain fame and power to influence decisions. This tension created by the two characters is materialized in the two background colors. The colors gray and blue, plastered side by side, evoke the idea of the existence of separate and opposed spaces, as well as the existence of interconnected spaces. The dividing line created by the two colors gives it a double meaning, since it can be understood as a demarcating line that separates the sides and thus makes explicit the antagonism between "heaven" and "hell." Also, as a thin and almost invisible thread between good and evil, it represents the dilemmas that many young people face in choosing paths and making life choices.

The boy's body stands between the angel and the devil, who culturally mobilize affect. The structure of the compositions reinforces the connections between prison and school. The body is placed slightly to the left and right, in the middle of a sloping and unstable line. The young man's expression, with his finger just below his mouth, suggests doubt and suspicion; he seems lost in thought, trying to decide which way to go. His body is facing the drawing on the image's right — school — but his back is to the left — crime — and being in the middle of the two indicates uncertainty: the advantage of staying close to the world of crime or choosing the school. Although he is inclined to the "good" side, school, the world of crime, "evil," tempts him. However, he is connected to both places by the line that can be metaphorically called "the razor's edge," which offers the boy both sides and leaves him halfway. He will always be in a struggle to choose one of the possibilities for the *hip-hop* cultural movement.

The written text below the images of the jail and school supports the visual elements. The images, combined with the title *Hip-Hop Educando*, are presented in large, solid dark letters on the left and right sides of the page. With the help of images and antagonistic words (demon and angel, prison and school), it is implied that *hip-hop* is a cultural movement that can make everyday life poetic without detaching itself from reality and the place where it comes from. On the CD cover, the set of verbal and non-verbal elements are ways to offer a piece of advice and an invitation to participate in the *hip-*

hop cultural movement from the perspective shown in the *rap* lyrics "Education is the motto."

Although in its social practices, the *hip-hop* movement does not make an apology for criminality, nor does it defend only school education; rather, it considers the existence and the power both paths have. It welcomes and negotiates from a perspective of education carved in the purposes of the collective. Informed by polyphonic voices, *hip-hop* positions itself in a third space that does not separate the two sides and builds a third one, without ignoring the battles of the complexity of the third space: the strategies of reexistence, approach, negotiation, the tense discussion between the established and the astute re-creation of tactics that reinvent and construct reexistence strategies in the third space. Neither center nor margin, neither school nor prison, it is a daily journey invested with double value: cultural and political.

It is in this arena of debate that the young *rappers* position themselves. In doing so, they bring the knowledge of the street and the knowledge they learn in school, showing their concept of education in *hip-hop* culture linked to their reality and the daily experiences they live. In this way, they value the social practices of their experiences as *rappers* and as agents of literacies of reexistence:

> Innumerable ways of playing and foiling the other's game, that is, the space instituted by others, characterize the subtle, stubborn, resistant activity of groups which, since they lack their own space, have to get along in a network of already established forces and representations. People have to make do with what they have. In these combatants' strategies, there is a certain art of placing one's blows, a pleasure in getting around the rules of a constraining space (De Certeau, 1994: 79).

The following chapter will allow us to situate these subjects as literacy agents who can tactically "play the game" inside and outside the group to which they belong. There, they constitute themselves as individuals with significant and distinctive paths in search of affirmation, empowerment and legitimation.

CHAPTER 5

BATTLES AS SPACES FOR PRACTICES OF REEXISTENCE

Like (+) because those who just started in *rap* don't know much/ they think it's just come and play a CD in the background and sing over it (+) this is not how it works/ (+) there's/ there's a whole te::::chnique. (+) you sing:::ing/ you rhym:::ing and /.../ we try to teach this in the workshops and also (+) to the *rap* groups that come to us/
(LGe)

et us now think about the formal setting of dialogue and ways to debate which allow us to identify the identity constructions of the activists in interaction with different communicative situations. What seems to be interesting here is the battle for language in the MCs defiant rhymes, in the interactions with pedagogy students and in the inventiveness, speed and agility that make up the aesthetic features of a *rapper*. They win the battles with their ideas: in the competitions, in the disputes and "being hype," "keeping themselves in the spotlight," or "on the top of it," that is, producing an effect that might bring them closer to the image of winners or warriors.

We will analyze excerpts from three moments that I identify in which the use of the word as a battle becomes more visible:

1. Battles between "bros";

2. Battle between educators;

3. Battle of ideas between literacy agents.

At no time do they cease to be brothers, educators or agents; there is no separation or detachment between these moments. Instead, when they organize themselves as such, they allow us to illustrate how they strategically "battle" for their identities according to the occasion.

At the heart of the word "battle" is the idea of fighting or struggling tenaciously to achieve something, to solve problems and create ways out. The notion of battle creates a semantic field in which the meanings of collision, conflict, struggle, contention, duel, encounter, attack, victory, defeat, death and life appear. The images constructed from this authorize the association of the concept with military tactics and refer to scenes in which opponents angrily confront each other struggling for something or some symbolic or material good. Using the battle as a metaphor to describe ways of interacting, taking ownership of the word, creating the frameworks, constructing self-images[45] and placing them in relation to others helps analyze how *rappers* build their identities and support them in different contexts.

The resonances of this metaphor in the social use of the language of *rapper* activists can be better heard through the notion of conceptual metaphor which, according to Lakoff and Johnson (2002), concerns the ways we culturally make use of linguistic expressions in order to "understand and experience one thing in terms of another" (47-8). Thinking about the *hip-hop* universe's approximation to the metaphorical concept of *discussion is war*, which refers to the sense that discussion involves the need to attack positions, defend yourself and win, is of particular interest. Far from being just sets of words, "metaphors are part of people's thinking processes" (Lakoff and Johnson, 2002: 49).

If we consider the perspective that arguing always involves fighting, war, a battle to plan and find ways of using words to confront

---

45   This is the notion of ethos from ancient rhetoric, now taken up by theories of enunciation and discourse analysis (Charaudeau, Maingueneau, 2004).

the other, De Certeau's (1994) definition of tactics is also pertinent to the discussion:

> /.../ "a calculus which cannot count on a "proper," nor thus on a borderline distinguishing the other as a visible totality. "The place of a tactic belongs to the other. A tactic insinuates itself into the other's place, fragmentarily, without taking it over in its entirety, without being able to keep it at a distance. It has at its disposal no base where it can capitalize on its advantages, prepare its expansions, and secure independence with respect to circumstances" (46-7).

A tactic is the vision of opportunities to act in the places, in the gaps through which, cunningly, those who perceive them pass and penetrate. "[A] tactic depends on time—it is always on the watch for opportunities that must be seized 'on the wing'. Whatever it wins, it does not keep" (De Certeau, 1994: 47). Hence the need to play with events to turn them into 'occasions' for success. Weakness must unceasingly take advantage of forces that are alien to it. In the tactical game, winning and possessing are instantaneous and elusive, so it depends on attention and discernment to move in the arena where we struggle with and for language, as we will see below in three moments when activists act tactically.

BATTLE BETWEEN "BROS": A RAPPER STYLE OF COMBAT

The activists consider holding workshops and lectures in schools as an opportunity to establish possible bridges between the appreciation (by them) and the devaluation (by society) of the literacies that *hip-hop* culture makes possible. These are also opportunities for the activists to present *hip-hop*, construct self- images and problematize prejudices, intolerances and stigmas concerning this cultural movement.

In the activities they conduct, they face rejection when, by entering the educational spaces, they bring issues that are indigestible to the great majority of the audience, as well as the "voices of the body" (De Certeau, 1994) that move social attributes and ways of speaking that are not accepted or that are socially devalued. These voices of the body challenge the cultural rules and bring their corporeality from minority groups — Black and poor, young people and residents of the *periferias* of the cities — as they are usually diminished and nullified by several biased mechanisms that reaffirm society's unwillingness to accept communicative styles that are not aligned with the Eurocentric — white and middle-class — standard.

The activists experienced this situation in a lecture they gave to education students in a private university in São Paulo. The goal was to present the *hip-hop* cultural movement as a possibility for education. The lecture was carefully planned; before the scheduled date, the group of activists held two preparatory meetings aimed at establishing objectives, selecting materials, resources and possible strategies for approaching the theme. Their aim was to find ways to use the word to succeed in their social communication, as shown in the excerpt from one of the meetings:

890 LGe: Dim, when we go to that university to lecture, we'll say: I think *hip-hop* is important for education

8191 Dimenor: Look, not like that, bro! We should say: *hip-hop* is important for education. It makes our position stronger.

The excerpt shows a concern to monitor not only what they are going to say, but also how they are going to work language to face the battle of convincing the speakers to build a positive image of the movement and the group, to strengthen themselves in front of the other and to secure the role of authorized speaker. Dimenor argues that instead of modularizing the statement, thus reducing their commitment to its truth — *I think hip-hop is important for education* — they should enunciate this commitment with an argument that presents a universal value — *hip-hop is important for education*. Being assertive is necessary when the weak ones are tactically set up on the ground of the strong ones to deliver their blows, as De Certeau (1994) puts it.

Even with the prior planning, the speakers showed concern in organizing their speech so that the education students could hear, consider and validate it. On the day of the presentation, the group traveled for about two hours, during rush hour traffic, which was considerably more intense because of the heavy rain in November.

They were very nervous when they arrived at the university. In the waiting room, they started a challenge game to relax. Departing from a specific theme, each one of them joined the circle, took the word and started rhyming on it.

In this communication situation, the verbal art is stamped in the battle; in the fight for the word, in the most *rapper*-style speech pattern, the fastest, most provocative, most dynamic and most creative wins. Victory is individual, the word needs to convey meaning. The *rapper* must elicit a response from the others and instigate a verbal challenge. He must know how to rhyme to be a good MC. By hearing, seeing and reading the movements of language in *hip-hop*, especially in the MCs' practices, it is possible to notice that the word appears as an engine of action for individuals that, through the language in operation, acts in world-making and constituting identities that are formed and transformed, as proposed by Hall (2003).

The MC, who speaks for the people from the *periferia*, plays a strategic role in narrating the daily experiences as rhymed poetry, as the wise man, the counselor or even as storytellers from the territories of Black and poor white people. These are the *brodas* and *sistahs* who, through their words, vocalize and echo the entanglement of voices of those discontented with the living conditions of a big part of the least favored section of the population.

Although the word in *hip-hop* is not unique and in unison, it has socio- historical inscriptions that affirm the MCs as collective speakers, always dealing with the social voices present as co-enunciators.

In the teachers' room, the word was used by the group when, before the lecture started, they decided to use the 15 minutes they had left to play with each other, test the camcorder and quarrel to see who handled the rhymes better.

Below is the transcription of an excerpt from a verbal challenge between Dimenor and LGe. It lasted about 4 minutes. I will analyze one minute of the excerpt, which illustrates Dimenor's speech in the battle for a good word. I will present the fragments twice.[46] First, the whole rap, in order to give an idea of the verse's rhythm, and then

---

46   See the table on Page 177 with the conventions used in transcription.

I will present it [next to its version in Portuguese] followed by an analysis.[47]

°yo, I got° <the GIFT of RHYme>(1.) >better believe<it	°aí. eu tenho° <o DOM da RIma>(1.) >pode acredi<tá
>dimenor from bristol park < coming (1.0) >for< it	>dimenor do parq bristol < chegou (1.0) >pa-ra<re- vo-lu-cio-nahha
come on [(xxxxx) distinct rhyming.] (.) my —self-esteem	vamos [(xxxxxx) a rima.] (.) diferente — a— autoestima
co°mes° qui°ckly though ain't slower than my, (.) phi-lo-so-phy	é ti°po° mais rá°pdə °ou mais lenta a minha, (.) fi- lo-so-fia
>Yo,< elegê, (.) stop watchin' me And come here to sing (.) GO learn some rhyming. (1.0) u know?	>então,< elegê, (.) para de me observá. e começa a cantar (.) VA aprendê a rimá. (1.0) morou?
here the constitution goes far be-yon::::d Singin', talking', rappin' I be around:d::	aqui a constituição vai muito mais alé::::m no cantado no falado no rap eu chegue:i::
>>Changing the rhyme<< ()is pretty cool(.) completeLY	>>mudando a rima<< ( )diferente (.) totalMENTE falô? (1.0) <otário.>
I'm off (1.0) <you fool.> our<° hands are full°>	é<°tu:do com a ge::nte°>

We can notice that the cadenced rhythm of the *rap* style, with alternations between the higher and lower pitches of voice, builds a movement that is proper to the struggle, the challenge, as when bodies get closer and more distant in confrontations. The idea of struggle for space is due to the notable alternation that the MC makes between stressed and non-stressed syllables, which are whispered (phonetically, [park] instead of [parki]). The tonic syllables, by contrast, sound stronger, or do not merge; for instance, they are pronounced without the abbreviations, as in *pa-ra* (and not *pra*, the common pronunciation in spoken Portuguese). In other cases, there is a separation of the article and the first syllable with the same sound, as in *a-autoestima* (self-esteem). We can say that the sounds alternate between stronger and weaker, thereby emulating

---

47   The same verse re-textualized from oral to written allows a more linear reading: Yo, I got the gift of rhyme, better believe it Dimenor from Bristol Park coming for it Come on (xxxxx) distinct rhyming, my self-esteem Comes quickly though ain't slower than my philosophy Yo LGe stop watching me And come here to sing with me Go learn some rhyming, you know? The constitution goes far beyond Singin', talking', rappin' I be around Changing the rhyme is pretty cool I'm off, you fool! Our hands are full

dance movements. It is stronger when approaching other sounds, and weaker when moving away, as in the challenges performed in capoeira circles.

In the verbal challenge, the verses are recited with intensity, sometimes speaking directly to the person being challenged — >Yo,< *elegê, (.) stop watchin' me and come here to sing (.) with me (.) GO learn some rhyming..* —, or by checking comprehension and asking for confirmation — u know —, which allows us to identify the activist's intention to show his ability to fit the right words together "without failing," and as if he were saying "that's how you rhyme." It is worth remembering that teaching how to *rap* is one of the most valued dimensions in *hip-hop*, especially for the activists participating in the research, who are engaged in organizing workshops for children, teenagers and other young people who also want to learn how to use words to express their worldviews.

In the second transcription of the excerpt, this time with my remarks, it is observed how, in addition to words, Dimenor uses his body to create the desired sonority in the challenge he makes to LGe. The following images are some of the frames taken from the DVD recording of the event to illustrate how the body movements follow the rhythm of the rap.

At the beginning of his speech, Dimenor calls his partner's attention by lowering his voice, almost whispering. He then raises his voice to announce his ability to rhyme and, at a faster pace, he requests the attention of others.

°yo, I got° <the GIFT of RHYming>(1.) ((raises his head looking at LGe in a challenging way)) >better believe<it ((shakes his head in affirmation))

Images 8–9

The moment he raises his voice to say that he has the gift of rhyming is relevant to the duel because knowing how to rhyme is crucial to an MC's path. In rap, the rhyme holds the listener's attention. Through quality, sonority and more or less appropriate metrics, the *rapper* shows the repertoire he possesses, as well as his ability to establish semantic relationships and argue convincingly through language.

Images 10-11

Another feature to highlight concerns his mention of the place he comes from:

>dimenor from bristol park < ((opens his eyes and looks at his peer)) coming (1.0) >for< it ((aspirating and making the syllable longer))

>*dimenor do parq bristol* < ((opens eyes, looks at colleague)) arrived (1.0) >*pa-ra<re-vo-lu-cio-nahha* ((aspirating and lengthening the syllable)).

He says he is from Bristol Park, which is the same as saying "I come from the *periferia*," with his voice quickening because this information is far from new to his peers. It loses relevance before the next statement, which he has carefully prepared. Dimenor opens his eyes a little more and looks at his partner as he organizes his performance to show himself as someone who has "an attitude," someone who is critical and has goals, someone who is able to act through words. In the following excerpt, his perception of the importance of language control stands out: *it co°mes° qui°ckly though ain't slower than my, (.) phi-lo-so-phy.* He demonstrates his metadiscoursal mastery by showing that he chooses the way to express his philosophy according to his intentionality:

>so,< choose, (.) stop watchin' me ((breaths in and brings his hands to his waist))

And starts singing (.) GO learn some rhyming. (1.0) u know?

Image 12

Again, he speaks with his body to reinforce his speech; he brings his hands to his waist, indicating his readiness for the confrontation that is about to unfold. He gives two orders to his partner: to stop watching him, and then, in a much louder voice, in relation to the previous context, he gives the second order, telling him to "learn" to rhyme, because, as it seems, his partner doesn't know how to do it yet. Then he begins to direct the end of the battle:

here ((points his right hand's index finger to the floor)) The constitution goes far beyon::::d ((with the arm and thumb of the hand pointing to his back))

Singin', talking', rappin' I be around:d::((points his index finger to himself)) I arrived:d:: >>>Changing the rhyme<< () is pretty cool.

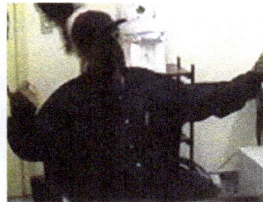

Images 13–14

Dimenor, when referring to the constitution, values it as a written document, as a symbol of power and reference, but he emphasizes that beyond the ability to read the written text, as a *rapper* he uses the rhyme because of his knowledge of orality. In this way, he sets the laws and codes of the constitution in motion. In this way, he begins to draw with his body the synthesis of the performance:

> Singin', talking', rappin' I be around:d:: ((points his index finger to himself))
>
> >>Changing the rhyme<< ()is pretty cool
>
> I'm off (1.0) <you fool.> ((gets closer and puts his face very close to LGe's face))
>
> our<° hands are full°> ((slaps LGe's chest and then slaps his own))

Images 15-17

Dimenor's body movements can be analyzed using the approach of proxemics, defined as "the study of human use of space as a specific product" (Hall, 1986: 132). The study of body movements allows us to understand that the ways of making connections with spaces are culturally maintained. The actions of the body, accompanied by verbal actions such as the tone and intensity of the voice, "are sources of information about the distance that separates two individuals" (p. 132). By observing how people position their bodies in situations such as standing in line or standing in a circle, Hall distinguishes differences in interactions according to the greater or lesser proximity of the body depending on its location and in relation to the other.

In the last images, we can see that the way Dimenor plays with the word is also accompanied by body language. In this case, the body emphasizes the *rapper*-style attitude, provocative, challenging, revealing the desired modes of interaction at the moment of the battle. The closer the better to support the word they want to emphasize.

Dimenor speaks very fast, then pauses briefly, creating a sense of curiosity, preparing the audience to hear about his ability to make a revolution out of his rhymes. To mark the scope or magnitude of the change, he fully emphasizes the last two syllables in the word *compleTELY*. In this way, he reaffirms the importance of being eloquent in verbal battles and in the search for arguments to support the word that, once said, must be heard, validated, magnified and answered in the midst of a verbal game that includes repetition, persistence and instigation.

The verbal game played in the waiting room was a "warm-up" for another battle arena, this time with people who are not *hip-hop* activists, but future educators. For about ten minutes, the *rappers* took turns fostering the collaborative production that served as a challenge and a manifestation of solidarity among the *rappers* who would soon enter another arena. This time, it was a new space of practice they didn't know.

BATTLES BETWEEN EDUCATORS: BEING LEGITIMATED IN A NEW SPACE OF PRACTICE

As the activists made their way to the lecture hall, they met briefly before entering the room. They discussed how to conduct the activity. Débora opened the conversation by saying that everyone talks too much and that they should be organized for the lecture and stick to the plan. They should avoid contradictions, respect the three minutes each had to speak, build consensus, and above all, avoid talking over or interrupting someone else's speech, as always happened in the discussion circles.

In the situation where the activists would speak to the education students, the battle was very different from the one they had experienced in the waiting room. The weapon was still language in action, but it is worth remembering that although they were the lecturers, there was a social asymmetry in a more concrete situation. The activists were the guests, but they occupied a socially inferior position compared to their listeners, who were university students. At the same time, they were trying to convince the audience to recognize them as educators and agents of literacy. We cannot overlook the interaction of social and institutional powers in the development of the meeting.

They organized themselves tactically to ensure the expected success, aware that their legitimacy as educators was in question, at least in the beginning.

In the room, after the initial greetings and their introductions, they began the presentation with an exhibition of a video about ten minutes long. It was about the four expressions of *hip-hop*: break dancing, graffiti, music and poetry. The students were in a rectangular room with chairs arranged in a semicircle. There were five young instructors, three sitting, one at the end of the table and one standing — some of them with paper to take notes. I sat at the back of the room as I was the professor in charge of the class.

After showing the video, Nathas asked in a high, paused voice if anyone wanted to ask a question. No one asked anything. Then he asked again, and since he had no answers, he introduced himself. Then each of the speakers introduced themselves, said their names and talked about the activities they had developed, as well as their views on *hip-hop*. The audience, almost in total silence, listened attentively.

Among all the speech, we will analyze Dimenor's speech again. It gives examples of some prosodic features that characterize the activists' discourse in this communicative situation where it was convenient for everyone to show shared knowledge about *hip-hop* and education. In this excerpt, the contrast in word usage is striking when compared to the previous verbal challenge. If previously the intended *ethos*[48] was that of a defiant warrior, in the excerpt we will show it is possible to notice the search for another ethos, that of an educator. Let us observe how the statements he makes in front of an audience attempt to reproduce presumed values and construct the desired meanings for *hip-hop*.

> Dimenor: ((leans back in his seat, raises his torso and moves forward to approach the audience)) °good evening°, °I am dimenor°, I'm part of the >*movimento enraizado*[49]<(.) youth organization that works (3') ((brings his arm back, then forward, then lowers it, accentuating the word and raising the volume of his voice)) For the social inclusion of the *periferia* of São Paulo >and some parts of Rio de Janeiro too<. This is the point of view we have as— (.) educationa::l *hip-hop* (1.0) in the <beginn::ing> there was *hip-hop*<marginaliZEd> which was a— (.) a concept very— (..) when you say marginalized, in my conception (.) it's a derogatory concept. (.) WHY? (.) when we—we say that *hip-hop* is marginalized it's not FOR (.) the thugs, crime, but because it's organized ((makes a circle with his hands)) at the margins of society (.) so it means (.) society excludes:: (.) the people, <the people from the *periferia*>, (.) the °people° from the slums, and we have no place to go for culture (.) and so *hip-hop* has been bringing this culture that is more in the center of the city down to the *periferia*, the slums. this is the point of view we have.

In addition to verbal communication, Dimenor uses his body as his "calling card" in what is a convention in *hip-hop*. He sits in a chair while speaking, facing the host audience side by side with his "ally" listeners. Before greeting the audience, he corrects his posture and puffs out his chest, trying to give the impression of a *nice brother*, noting his intention as a speaker, as he was also an educator, to get

48   According to Maingueneau, "the text is not meant to be contemplated, it is an utterance addressed to a co- speaker who must be mobilized to physically adhere to a particular universe of meaning. The persuasive power of speech is largely due to the fact that it makes the reader identify with the movement of a body invested with historically determined values" (Maingueneau 2005, 73).
49   T.N.: Rooted movement.

"face to face" with his audience of educators. He then introduces himself saying:

good evening°, °I am dimenor°, I'm part of the >*movimento en-raizado*<(.) youth organization that works

Images 18-21

We notice that he alternates the rhythm and pitch of his voice, first lower and faster to minimize personal aspects, then more paused and louder to emphasize a characteristic of the *hip-hop* movement, which is, after all, the central theme of the presentation.

Then he points out the purpose of the movement to which he belongs — for *the social inclusion of the periferias* — and again prosody and body movement work together: he quickly raises and lowers his arm and raises his voice to mark the place of affirmation.

With his speech and gestures, Dimenor brings a *rapper's style* to this communicative situation: he invests in body movements to emphasize and highlight the forcefulness of the speech. Gestures are typical MC actions when they *rap* on stage and want to emphasize the chorus of the songs, or even when activists participate in lectures or workshops.

Image 22

Then, the young man that is in solidarity with his group says: This is the point of view we have as— (.) educationa::l hip-hop (1.0) in the <beginn::ing> there was hip-hop<marginaliZEd>. When he states his point of view and uses the pronoun "we," he is affirming that Nathas, Débora, LGe and Soneca share the same perspective. We can understand the first pause he makes as a strategy to find the best way to tell the education students that, for them, hip-hop can educate and is therefore an "educational tool."

Image 23 — Lecture for pedagogy students © Domênica Sabino de Souza

It is possible to interpret a second pause as a slowing resource to plan his speech or to help him search for something important in his memory. The pause allows Dimenor, in a slower manner, to support Soneca's previous statement with new arguments. He thus refutes the idea of marginality that is part of the common sense of the majority of society: *so I am going to offer you a new vision of hip-hop, for many it is marginalized, understand? (.) and hip-hop(.) isn't — it is not marginalized, it takes people out of marginalization, understand? (.) an instrument to take people out of marginalization.* By revoicing Soneca, Dimenor shows collaboration and solidarity with his peers.

In this context, the reintroduction of information is a pedagogical resource that helps the teacher to work didactically and ideologically in front of the audience of students. He continues to do this when he uses a rhetorical question to emphasize what he considers important, which is to say that being marginalized does not mean being a criminal but being on the margins of society: *when you say marginalized, in my conception (.) it's a derogatory concept. (.) WHY? (.) when we—we say that hip-hop is marginalized it's not FOR (.) the thugs, crime, but because it's organized ((makes a circle with his hands)) at the margins of society.*

He continues: *society excludes:: (.) the people, <the people from the periferias>, (.) the °people° from the favelas, and we have no place to go for culture (.) and so hip-hop has been* decenTRAliZIng *this culture that is more in the center of the city down to the suburbs, to the favelas. this is the point of view we have.* The repetition of the word *people* three times – *(.) the people, <the people of the periferia>, (.) <the ° people° from the favela>* — marks his opposition to the hegemonic society. He is also part of the people, but as a *hip-hop* activist, he is closer to those who live on the margins of society and seek education in and through culture. His emphasis on the word decenTRAliZIng seems to mean the urgency, or the relevance, of better distribution and circulation of social productions.

They all took turns speaking and opening spaces for the others to share their thoughts. This shows that they have formed an alliance that subordinates the word to the objectives of the speakers involved in the new communication context. That is, to balance the power relations imbricated in the situation.

Image 24 — Lecture for pedagogy students — © Domênica Sabino de Souza

This was different from what happened in the intra-group inter-action before the lecture — an interaction between friends, almost intimate, since the battle was between *hip-hop* members. They were more defiant and spontaneous. They battled in a *rapper*'s style. But in the context of the lecture, they used more formal words, redefined some of them, exchanged glances and spoke slowly.

The young activists show that they use the spoken word in the struggle for a space among educators who still kept their socio-historical features in orality, rhythm and repetition. Through their speech, they sought to constitute themselves as educators both for themselves and for others. In this case, the gestures and speech with different rhythms and intonations take place in a concrete situation according to the ideological investment of the group. They planned how to use language: how will others see me; how should I construct my speech? How should I behave, how should I sit, what gestures should I make? In addition, they redefined vocabulary and made lexical choices to maintain the *ethos* of authority, the one who knows how and what to say to subvert ideas about young Black *rappers* and even about what can be understood as education. Such possibilities of planning and the lexical choices can be characterized as evidence of the effects of being into *hip-hop*, an important literacy agency for their identity constitution. In the next section, we will see another tactical use of language, focusing on excerpts from two *rodas de conversa* where battles over ideas are present between literacy agents.

BATTLE OF IDEAS BETWEEN LITERACY AGENTS FOR THE MEANINGS OF WORDS

One of the principles of *hip-hop* culture is to attribute the power of action and transformation to language use, which aims to carefully disseminate worldviews and behaviors in the battle for the meanings that are constituted at the intersection of social voices.

We will analyze an excerpt from the first *roda de conversa* when we discussed their reading preferences. At a certain point, the race issue became so important that we decided it deserved its own space. In that sense, the second *roda* was primarily about it.

In the interactive universe of the discussion circles, we encountered three voices. Of course, there were tensions and asymmetries. The first is *hip-hop*, represented by the group of young activists who, in this scenario, were invested with values, a set of practices and viewpoints, and recognized themselves as fundamental participants in the process of data generation. The second is the academic, represented by me, my values, worldviews and positions to achieve the goals I set for the research. The third corresponds to the intellectuals and social activists, where I situate myself with the participants. We assume the role of activists engaged in alternative educational projects meant to raise awareness of racial and social differences in order to overcome the racial discrimination that historically shape the struggle for rights.

The following excerpts are part of the first *roda de conversa*, which took place in August 2004, when the young participants showed their reading collections.[50]

Image 25 — Roda de conversa in August 2004 — © Analu

528 Q: By the way/ the book is the::: ?

529 LGe: *Jogo duro* by Elias ((unintelligible))/ Hugo Correia//

---

50   The use of bold letters in the transcription serves only to draw attention to the fact being analyzed.

530 Q: That one was//

531 LGe: Once upon a time there was a::: the history of **Black** people (.) that was **whitewashed** / (.) do you un derstand? (.) and I brought this book because (.) it ques tions Princess Isabel/ (.) who they say freed **Black** people, right/ they say that::: right/ here with simple words/ with some drawings/ they simplify it a lot/ (.) they sim plify because:: (.) he talks about the victory of **Black people**/ that didn't only have a **Black** man as a hero/ didn't have only the *Quilombo dos Palma:::res*/ (.) be cause a majori::ty/ (.) like (+) an entire continent be comes enslaved (.) by the hands of half a dozen **whites**/ (.) **he makes this very (+) dark** for us to understand/

532 Q: ((laughter))

533 Dimenor: Instead of being **very clear**/ **very dark**/ that's right/

534 LGe: A:::H and another thing, and this book is also **very dark** about that word... bu::t is /.../ like this / (.) **neguinho**[51] did i::t/ **neguinho** did tha::t/ things look pret ty **Black** for me/ etc./ etc./ etc./

535 Soneca: That's it/ like saying the you're the **Black** sheep of the family/

536 LGe: Yes/ these things/

537 Soneca: that's why he said **clear**/ **dark**//

538 LGe: a::: we (.) it's this expla /.../ it's the (.) this book makes this ve::ry (.) explicit right/ and it also talks about why the (.) the enslaved one were the Bla::ck (.) and not the Indigenous people

Defining yourself or the other as Black, afro-Brazilian, *neguinho*, *pretinho*, whitey, mobilizes and confronts their views, thus producing varied effects:

---

51   T.N.: *Neguinho* is a Brazilian Portuguese word associated with a racial slur in Brazil that can be translated as "nigga." The word is often used as a diminutive form of "negro" (Black) in informal speech in Brazil. While its literal translation can mean "little black," it is essential to understand that the term is laden with historical and contemporary racial and social implications, and its usage can be highly problematic. The acceptability of this term can vary widely depending on the context, relationship between speakers and regional differences within Brazil. Some individuals may use it colloquially within their communities, while others may find it offensive.

531 LGe: Once upon a time there was a::: the history of **Black** people (.) that was whitewashed / (.) do you understand? (.) and I brought this book because (.) it questions (.) Princess Isabel/ (.) who they say freed Black people, right/ they say that::: right/ here with simple words/ with some drawings/ they simplify it a lot/ (.) they simplify because:: (.) it is about the victory of **Black people**/ that didn't only have a **Black** man as a hero/

First of all, it is an explicit adherence to the discourse of Black movements in Brazil, which have long been vocal about the fact that the "liberation" of enslaved people in the country in 1888 was only for show. In the socio-historical context of the early 21st century, this point of view is not only present in the speech of activists, albeit sometimes in a distorted way, but it's also incorporated into the social imagination of the Brazilian people. However, in this same excerpt, we can find conflicting voices regarding the same Black movements when it comes to self-denomination, *preto* or *negro*.[52]

Today, the use of the expression *raça negra* [Black race], widely employed in contexts of activism and incorporated by academia, focuses on the social and political dimensions of racism, considering that its existence in society still marks and places hierarchies among different groups. This causes serious damages that are more visible to Black people — *pardos* and *pretos*. LGe's discourse, when referring to the book *Jogo Duro* [Rough Game], opposes the slogan widely spread by Black movements since the 1980s: *negro é raça, preto é cor*.[53]

By affirming to be *preto*, the *rapper* not only places himself in opposition to the *movimentos negros* [Black movements] but also concerns the ideology of whitening or the idea of *moreno Brasil*, a kind Black person. In general, for *hip-hop*, the category "*negro*" is an academic

---

52   T.N.: In Brazil, the terms *'preto'* or *'negro'* are used to refer to Black people. There is an ongoing debate about whether Black Brazilians should identify as *negros/as* or *preto/as*. Decades ago, referring to Black Brazilians as *pretas/os* was considered a racial slur. Today, the term has been resignified and is widely used. According to the IBGE (Brazilian Institute of Geography and Statistics), Black people make up more than 56% of the Brazilian population, and the percentage of the category represents the sum of people who self- identify as *pretas/os* and *pardas/os*. The categories *preta* and *parda* are used by IBGE to classify dark skinned people (*pretas*) and mixed-raced or light skinned people (*pardas*). In this sense, *pardos* (mixed-race) would be considered "*negros*" in the Brazilian context.
53   T.N.: This slogan resonates with the discussion in the previous footnote. "*Negro é raça, preto é cor*" literally means "*negro* is race, *preto* is a color."

concept that refers to an educated Black middle class conforming to certain standards that they want no association to. This question takes us back to what I discussed in the methodology chapter when I talked about the reluctance of some collectives to accept my invitation to participate in the research. In this way, even though LGe was establishing a dialogue with those other voices, he kept some distance and introduced himself using the term *preto*. He thus denotes that his identity as a *rapper* is more important than being "*negro.*" Although in that conversation we could see the importance of this movement, because the voices of academia and Black and white *rappers* were all together, it is not often that the activists can make this distinction so explicitly and politically. Let's remember that *hip-hop* has been heavily influenced by the ideas of the Black movement [*movimento negro*], so the personal and collective identity affiliation is undeniable.

Gradually, the positions and lexical choices allow us to see that what is at stake is the struggle for terminology, to ensure the social identity of *rappers* not only in front of the elite and society in general but also within the larger overview of Black social movements. At the heart of the battle is the idea of making efforts not only to defeat the opponent but also to overcome and demonstrate your abilities to yourself.

As in battles and other *hip-hop* tactics, these actions in the art of doing multiply and can circumscribe places and roles for individuals. Being a part of the *hip-hop* movement, as defined by the research participants, requires speaking out, exposing your ideas and convincing others through speech. Therefore, the different terminologies you choose to compose discourse are not simple ways to speak, but ways of taking positions in specific scenarios.

The search for the articulation of the socio-historical aspects that need to be expressed appears in the battle, in which images are tactically constructed. This can be observed in terms that we find in the interactions we are analyzing here. The *rapper's* identity lies in showing that he knows how to use the word, but not just any word. Using a selected word is a requirement for reinforcing the ritualization of belonging to the *hip-hop* universe, which, in conversation with other discourse, aims to create a powerful place.

They continued the conversation, this time being ironic about the use of an ordinary word in the daily life of Brazilians. The word also allowed them to reveal the clash of social voices.

> 534 LGe: A:::H and another thing, and this book is also very dark about that word (++) bu::t is /.../ like this (+) neguinho did i::t/ neguinho did tha::t/ things look pretty black for me/ etc./ etc./ etc./
>
> 535 Soneca: That's it/ like saying the black sheep of the family/
>
> 536 LGe: Yes/ these things/
>
> 537 Soneca: that's why he said clear/ dark//
>
> 538 LGe: a::: we (+) it's this expla — it's the (+) this book makes this ve::ry (+) explicit right — and it also talks about why the (+) the enslaved were the Bla::ck (.) and not the Indigenous people

The play on words occurs when LGe brings the voice of a society that discriminates and diminishes minority groups. He immediately disqualifies it, thus promoting the effect of a sense of denunciation of racist and prejudicial practices impregnated in the language we use. This is present in the sense of "becoming intelligible" that the word "clear" brings. By creating a field of tension with other social and racial voices, the activist undermines this meaning, because the expression "very dark" contradicts the discourse of each and every Portuguese speaker, a language that, like many others, carries in its core the idea that the color white is enlightening and associated with good things. When it comes to Black people, it is common to use expressions that associate the color black with bad things or situations. So when he uses phrases like n*eguinho did this / neguinho did that /* or *things look pretty black to me*, he is satirizing the white racist voices. When he makes fun of the commonsense discourse, which is racist in its very structure, LGe makes the members of the circle laugh. By turning language inside out, he demonstrates that when "loaded" with ideology, it can be stripped of its veil of apparent transparency and neutrality as well as giving voice to discourses that aim to deconstruct the naturalized idea of language use. Understanding the discourses on race relations in the set of statements requires approaching a complex set of labels that are historically and socially constructed, materialized in voices that are intertwined in the struggle to produce meaning.

We have seen that an analysis of the designations requires considering the ideological aspects present in their use at the moment of speech. It also necessitates considering the clash that the labels create with other social voices whose categories are challenged by the activists, such as race, class and ethnicity. In this sense, this particular excerpt reiterates fundamental issues in the history of the relations built between white and Black people in Brazil, and also between Black people who are part of different social movements.

The excerpts from the second *roda de conversa*, which we will now analyze, focus on how activists negotiate and debate the meanings of words. The statements show how naming is inextricably linked to the identities and experiences of the individuals.

In the first excerpt, we see how activists position themselves regarding the presence of Black people in the media. This issue is closely related to their identities as *hip-hop* activists, because the more *hip-hop* gains ground in public events, the more the media becomes interested in this phenomenon, which attracts audiences, among other things. Participation in the media is not easy among activists, even if we are talking about Black people in general and not just those who are part of the *hip-hop* movement. Let's look at the following excerpt:

898 LGe: Don't you want to explain? //

899 Q: And what was the controversy again? (+) I heard the topic/ (+) I remember the topic was (+) **Black people in the media**//

900 LGe: **It was a victory**

901 Dimenor: **Or manipulation**//

902 LGe: **Success**//

903 P: **Success/ victory**//

904 Soneca: **Manipulation or (deception)**//

905 LGe: No/ because it ain't no victory/ (+) no victory/ ((several voices))

906 P: WELL/ it started like this/ Black people in the Media/ then there was//

In the statements, we observe provocations in relation to the possibilities of greater or lesser success in the argumentation. Being prepared, or not, for the *roda de conversa*, which Dimenor calls a court, is a metaphor that refers to judging different versions of the same issue.

It is interesting to focus on one aspect of the *roda de conversa* from the beginning, the conflict that occurs when the activists expose different opinions. One after another, they use the words: *manipulation*, *deception*, *victory* and *success*. They tried to give a direction to this controversial discussion. They tried to battle to impose a "single" point of view. It was not by chance that when I introduced the topic, I called it a controversial topic. I recalled that in the previous *circle*, the topic had provoked a heated debate and gained such a dimension that we chose it as the focus of the next meeting. Even before the topic "Black people in the media" was introduced, they remembered it as something that had generated discussions and debates and created controversy among them. For this reason, the circle was considered a court. After trying to establish some "order" to start the debate, it was interesting to realize that the activists were concerned with establishing an argumentative course for the topic. In the discursive follow-up, we can understand that the presence of Black people in the media is a result of previous struggles. A history or a struggle that had a "winner" after many attempts. At first, it seems that achievement, which refers to the process, and victory, which reminds us of the result, illustrates this history more clearly. But manipulation and deception resignify the process.

They play a game in which two things must occur:

- Someone is deceived and allowed to be deceived.
- Someone deceives.

In the *roda de conversa*, or court, the young people invested in the use of language to put their point of view, battling to have a turn to speak and a voice to impose ideas that would "set the tone" of the conversation.

In the course of the debate, the activists use repetition, both to dispute the turn and to give a certain rhythm to the *roda de conversa*. In addition, it is important to notice the use of jargon specific to the *periferic* identity they claim.

> 907 LGe: Let me/ just say something, Soneca (.) like (.) like (.) I agree with what you said (.) the only thing I disagree with is the word WINNING (.) because we win nothing
>
> b908 Soneca: **You're confusing things**.
>
> 909 LGe: **I ain't confusing nothing**.
>
> 910 Soneca: You won from Black people, my friend (.) I am not saying that white people just thew it at our hands (.) you don't understand the *bagulho*[54] (.) you can't understand the *parada*

It is interesting to observe how the turns are chained with the almost literal restatement of what the other said, thus creating a rhythm, a sonority represented in excerpts like these: *you are confusing the bagulho / I'm not confusing anything /.../ you don't understand the parada / I understand perfectly /.../ you don't understand / of course I do.*

In the battle for significance, one cannot use just any vocabulary. Not only do the mentioned words mark critical positions — *success, victory, manipulation, deception* — but also indicate from which social position the activists talk: *bagulho, parada, tá ligado*. They show they are discussing the issue as *rappers*, Black and poor individuals from the *periferia*. That is why they can't use any word, but a selected lexicon that needs to make sense. It is still possible to observe that reinstating what the other said constitutes a clash in the sense of who can understand or not; who is confused and who is not. It represents a duel to establish who they are in the circle to establish which idea will win. The battle for the meanings of Black people being in the media is still important: *winning, achieving, manipulating and accomplishing.*

---

54   T.N.: In Brazilian Portuguese slang, "bagulho" and "parada" are informal terms that can have different meanings depending on the context. In the context mentioned here the words mean "thing." Both "bagulho" and "parada" are informal expressions and may vary in meaning depending on the region and context in which they are used. They are commonly heard in everyday conversation among young people in Brazil and may not be suitable for formal or professional contexts. It's important to be aware that slang terms can change in meaning over time and may have different interpretations in different regions of Brazil.

Being in the world of *hip-hop* and being part of it implies bringing the battle for ideas and words into the interaction. That indicates a *sui generis* manner to establish a dialogue. The way the theme has been taken up, through a lexicon related not only to the culture but also to its interactions with Black movements, establishes the *circle* as another space of identity constitution in which the speakers draw the power of their words, thus bringing the *voices from the margins* (Hall, 2003: 338). These are voices that, infused with values embodied by the one who speaks, battle for the images that they want to legitimate in a concrete situation.

In the search for an affirmation of being a *rapper*, the individuals use tactics to delimitate the territory. By doing so, they emphasize the strength of this position through repetition, rhythm, irony and naming. The requirement of a firm position, a strong one that resembles a warrior, does not allow modularization and, therefore, we always encounter direct, combative and emphatic speech. The battle in the excerpts conveyed in this last analysis allows us to affirm that the *rodas de conversa* were an exercise of investigation and struggle to occupy positions to legitimize their words.

FINAL THOUGHTS

"Letra é treta"
Allan da Rosa[55]

Hip-Hop, Education and Literacies of Reexistence seeks to characterize the *hip-hop* cultural movement as an agency of literacies and the activists as agents of literacy. From a socio-historical perspective, it is clear that the singular literacies assigned to the group participating in the research allowed them to redefine their identities, resignifying the roles and social locations assigned to them by a society marked by racial and social inequalities.

I seek to answer a question related to all the others, that is therefore central: Can we say "literacies of resistance," since the literacy practices and events of these young people are related to their contesting identities?

The answer to this question turned out to be affirmative and, in a way, began to be obtained from the first contact with the participating subjects. The research process, especially in terms of methodological issues, proved to be even more challenging because the participants, by questioning the quite disrespectful treatment they receive from parts of the academy, positioned themselves as individuals, demanded commitment, feedback, active participation and forged what I call *literacies of reexistence*. The very interaction with the activists ended up imposing a different way of doing research and gave this work a new configuration. The work, which initially aimed to think about these young people's reading and writing prac-

55   Allan da Rosa is an award-winning Black poet, writer, actor and historian based in São Paulo, Brazil.

tices as a resistance to school literacy, gradually became an invitation to enter a universe that was not limited to marking a contested position in song lyrics and engaged speech. In addition, the young people wanted their work, which was not limited to MC'ing, to be recognized as an instance of education and transformation.

In this sense, it was no longer a matter of observing the singularities of their literate practices, even if they were outside the school environment, but recognizing the extent to which they were not only literate, but also reformulated the viewpoint of the results, showing that they not only valued the school literate culture — although they refuted it in many moments — but above all, they reinvented, reformulated, redefined and practiced it. They not only resisted an exclusionary model of literacy supported by already crystallized forms of legitimation, but created other ways of saying what has already been said, indelibly marking their social identities. Hence the name literacies of *reexistence* instead of just "resistance."

The first three chapters allow us to glimpse how, in literacies of reexistence, literate discourse and practices give visibility to a socially invisible segment — mostly made up of Black men, women and young people living in the urban outskirts and those who attend public schools. The assertion of their social identities in spaces that historically delegitimize their culture, such as schools, universities or even downtown São Paulo, already represents a challenge to homogenization. Considering the history of the Black population in Brazil beyond resisting, it is also necessary to re-exist through language, imposing a different writing, another orality that is literate and that can go in the opposite direction of the various statistics regarding the Black population in the literacy universe presented in Chapter 1.

It is also noteworthy that the re-emerging literacies of *hip-hop* culture dialog with a moment in which schooling is being put in check: there is a gap between school and contemporary society. Among other things, there is the fact that the school has not been able to recognize and legitimize the presence of other cultures and other literacies already present in school life. They are present in the students' speech, gestures, clothing, themes and ways of speaking concerning socio-historical forms, revealing social and cultural patterns of language use that are important in everyday actions.

As explained in Chapters 2 and 4, by using language intentionally and with goals that are set according to the need to make decisions for action, the activist supports the Bakhtinian view of language, that we can only think about language in social and cultural contexts in a dialogical way. Dialogic is not a complement, but inherent to language itself. The moment I was analyzing the statements and the enunciation scene in the *rodas de conversa*, and also the materials the young participants brought, I realized how much this Bakhtinian framework comes into play when we refer to the literacy practices of *hip-hop*. Why reading? What are the goals of my speech? What themes are relevant to my life and community? Why and to whom should language be used and produced? The activists themselves answered these questions: *To shock!*

This book shows the complexity of literacies as individuals discover, locate, point, propose, act and teach others to act amid cultural and political activities, in interactions and through language. When they do so, they reinvent the literacies in *hip-hop*, which combines the literacies of life and school. As we saw in the *rap* lyrics *Education is the motto* in Chapter 4, school is contested, but also displaced in their favor when they manage to reevaluate the institution and give it social meanings.

By reinventing linguistic practices, activists establish creative ways of reading, speaking and interacting, just as they constitute reading collections when they invest in learning about themselves as well as their ethnic, racial and social belongings. This knowledge also circulates through their productions. From the CD cover to the fanzine, rap, battles, organization of events and graffiti, they imprint and reaffirm the collective nature of knowledge production. When they share their productions, they become literacy agents and trainers to other agents. This democratization of knowledge involves planning, knowing the "audience," using the most appropriate language modality for each person and being concerned to make themselves understood and to convince others. This is not only in relation to the content conveyed, but also in relation to their own image as a reader, activist, agitator and literacy agent, which is conflated with the image of the movement itself.

The literacies of reexistence do not happen suddenly, mainly because belonging to this movement means accepting some contracts established in the interactions and self-training sessions that the group promotes. It is a self- regulated action due to the need to give answers to the challenges posed by the center, postmodernity and crises. They do this using the Internet, recyclable printing, partnering with groups with similar goals (social movements, NGOs) and creating new methods for communication and interaction.

Observing the dynamics and multiple social uses of language, to build a bridge between what is inside and outside the classroom that allows the consideration of the different voices and identities that circulate in educational spaces, is one of the increasingly urgent tasks for school as an institution. This concern is significant at this socio-historical moment when the politics of education for all are emerging as key issues for a changing world, of which school is a part. We need to recognize and validate different practices of social language use as part of the cultural repertoire of new subjectivities.

Chapter 5 also makes explicit the literacies of reexistence and the agency of the individuals in three different situations of interaction, where they had to be concerned with the ways they used words to communicate their identities as *rappers*, educators and activists. Tactically, they use the ways of expressing their socio-historical affiliations through the evaluative appreciation implied in the chosen lexicon, the intonation, the rhythm of the word and the body.

In Chapter 5, we also observe that through speech, the participants bring into play and negotiate the identities that distinguish them as literacy agents within and outside their communities. The verbal and bodily utterances that show linguistic-discursive signs allow us to analyze how the different identity positions are built. Thus, when young people used language, they did so based on their socio-historical attributes, seeking to assert certain identity traits circumscribed in their discursive practices. Discourse is therefore part of a larger social structure and impacts that same structure.

Some members of this group stated that, among other things, being part of the movement allows them to act as protagonists in events in which language use, in its oral and written modalities, is central: composing *rap* lyrics, attending lectures, reading several texts such as newspapers, magazines and books, especially those that deal with the history of Black people in Brazil and around the world.

According to them, these practices effect significant changes in their way of acting and placing themselves concerning knowledge production. In activities outside school, they concretely engage with language, and, in real communication contexts, the recognition of themselves as literacy agents compels them to go beyond and join the different spaces of literacy to challenge themselves and test their abilities to learn to reaffirm the emerging literacies, the literacies of reexistence.

The data and analysis obtained from this study reveal a small part of the diversity of literacy practices existing in Brazil, as well as the wide disparities among groups based on social origin, education, profession, age, gender and race. They also show that there is a real need to understand this complexity and, above all, the possibilities for change within the literacy practices of the subject participants.

BIBLIOGRAPHY

Abramo, H. W., O uso das noções de adolescência e juventude no contexto bra-sileiro. In: *Juventude e adolescência no Brasil — referências conceituais*. São Pau-lo: Ação Educativa, 2005.

Abromavay, M. et al., *Gangues, galeras, chegados e rappers; juventude, violência e cidadania nas cidades da periferia de Brasília*. Rio de Janeiro: Garamond, 1999.

Abromovay, M., Castro, M. G., *Ensino médio: múltiplas vozes*. Brasília: UNESCO, MEC, 2003.

Albuquerque, C., *O eterno verão do reggae*. São Paulo: Editora 34, 1997. Alves, C., *Pergunte a quem conhece: Thaíde*. São Paulo: Labortexto, 2005. Amorim, M., A contribuição de Mikhail Bakhtin: a tripla articulação ética, esté-

tica epistemológica, in: Freitas, M. T. A; Jobim, S.; Kramer, S. (orgs.),

Ciências humanas e pesquisa; leituras de Mikhail Bakhtin. São Paulo: Cortez, 2003.

___, *O pesquisador e seu outro: Bakhtin nas ciências humanas*. São Paulo: Musa Edi-tora, 2004.

Amossy, R., O *ethos* na intersecção das disciplinas: retórica, pragmática, sociologia dos campos, in: Amossy, R. (org.), *Imagens de si no discurso: a construção do* ethos. São Paulo: Contexto, 2005.

Andrade, E. N., *Movimento negro juvenil: um estudo de caso de jovens rappers de São Bernardo do Campo*. (Mestrado). São Paulo: USP, 1996.

___, *Hip-hop*: movimento negro juvenil, in: Andrade, E. N., *Rap e educação. Rap é educação*. São Paulo: Selo Negro (Summus), 1999.

Andrews, G. R., *Negros e brancos em São Paulo: (1888-1988)*. Bauru: Edusc, 1998.

Araujo, C. A. M. et al., *Cidades negras: africanos, crioulos e espaços urbanos no Brasil escravista do século XIX*. São Paulo: Alameda Casa Editorial, 2008. Araújo, M., Silva, G., Da interdição escolar às ações educacionais de sucesso: escolas dos movimentos negros e escolas profissionais técnicas e tecnológicas, in: Romão, J., *História da educação do negro e outras histórias*. Brasília: Ministério da Educação. Secretaria de Educação Continuada, Alfabetização e Diversidade, 2005.

Azevedo, A. M. G., Silva, S. J. Os sons que vêm das ruas, in: Andrade, E. N.(org.), *Rap e educação. Rap é educação*. São Paulo: Selo Negro(Summus), 1999, p. 65-82.

Austin, J. L., *Quando dizer é fazer*. Porto Alegre: Artes Médicas, 1990. Bakthin, M./Voloshinov, V. N. ([1929], *Marxismo e filosofia da linguagem*. São Paulo: Hucitec, 1995.

Bakthin, M., *Estética da criação verbal*. São Paulo: Martins Fontes, 2003.

Barros, S. A. P., Discutindo a escolarização da população negra em São Paulo entre o final do século XIX e início do século XX, in: Romão, J., *História da educação do negro e outras histórias*. Brasília: Ministério da Educação. Secretaria de Educação Continuada, Alfabetização e Diversidade, 2005.

Barros, D. L. P., Fiorin, J. L., *Dialogismo, polifonia e intertextualidade*. São Paulo: Edusp, 1994.

Barton, D., Hamilton, M., Ivanic, R. (orgs.), *Situated Literacies: Reading and Writing in Context*. Londres: Routlege, 2000.

Barton, D., Hamilton, M., Práticas de letramento, in: Barton, D., Hamilton, M., Ivanic, R. (orgs.), *Situated Literacies: Reading and Writing in Context*. London: Routledge, 2000.

Bauman, Z., *Identidade*. Rio de Janeiro: Zahar, 2005.

Blass, L. M. S., *Estamos em greve! Imagens, gestos e palavras do movimento dos bancários, 1985*. São Paulo: Hucitec, 1992.

Bento, M. A. S., Carone, I. (orgs.), *Psicologia social do racismo: estudos sobre branquitude e branqueamento no Brasil*. Petrópolis: Vozes, 2002.

Bernd, Z., *Literatura e identidade nacional*. Porto Alegre: EdUFRGS, 1992. Bezerra, P., Poliofonia, in: Brait, B. (org.), *Bakhtin: conceitos-chave*. Belo Horizonte: Editora da UFMG, 2000, p. 333-382.

Bhabha, H. K., *O local da cultura*. Belo Horizonte: Editora da UFMG, 1998.

Brasil. *Lei 10.639/03, de 9 de janeiro de 2003*. Altera a Lei 9.394, de 20 de dezembro de 1996. D.O.U. de 23 de dezembro de 1996.

Brasil, Ministério da Educação. *Diretrizes Curriculares Nacionais e para a Educação das Relações Étnico-raciais e para o Ensino de História e Cultura Afro-Brasileira e Africana*. CNE/CP 003/2004, de 10 de março de 2004.

Bruner, J., Weisser, S., A invenção do ser; a autobiografia e suas formas, in: Olson, D. R., Torrance, N. (org.), *Cultura, escrita e oralidade*. São Paulo: Ática, 1995.

Bunzen, C. S., *Dinâmicas discursivas na aula de português: usos de livro didático e projetos didáticos autorais e construção de sentido*. (Doutorado). Campinas: IEL/UNICAMP, 2009.

Caldeira, T. P. R., *A política dos outros. O cotidiano dos moradores da periferia e o que pensam do poder e dos poderosos*. São Paulo: Brasiliense, 1984.

Cameron, D., Frazer, E., Harvey, P., Rampton, M. B. H., Richardson, K., *Researching Language. Issues of Power and Method.* Londres: Routledge, 1992.

Canclini, N. G., *Culturas híbridas — estratégias para entrar e sair da modernidade.* Rio de Janeiro: EDUSP, 2005.

Carboni. F., Maestrio, M., *A linguagem escravizada, língua, história, poder e luta de classes.* São Paulo: Expressão Popular, 2003.

Cardoso, M. N., *O movimento negro em Belo Horizonte: 1978-1998.* Belo Horizonte: Mazza Edições, 2002.

Cardoso, P. J. F., A vida na escola e a escola da vida: experiências educativas de afrodescendentes em Santa Catarina no século XX, in: Romão, J., *História da educação do negro e outras histórias.* Brasília: Ministério da Educação. Secretaria de Educação Continuada, Alfabetização e Diversidade. 2005.

Cavalleiro, E., *Do silêncio do lar, ao silêncio escolar.* São Paulo: Contexto, 2000.

Cavallo, G., Chartier, R., *História da leitura no mundo ocidental,* vol. I. São Paulo: Ática, 1998.

De Certeau, M., *A invenção do cotidiano: artes de fazer.* Petrópolis: Vozes, 1994.

Cezerilo, A. A. Q. dos S., *Irmandades negras: outro espaço de luta e resistência (1870-1890).* São Paulo: Annablume, 2002.

Charaudeau, P., Maingueneau, D., *Dicionário de análise do discurso.* São Paulo: Contexto, 2004.

Chartier, R., *Formas e sentido cultura escrita: entre distinção e apropriação.* Campinas: Mercado de Letras, Associação de Leitura do Brasil (ALB), 2003., *A história cultural: entre práticas e representações.* Lisboa: Difel, 1990.

Coimbra, C. M. B, O atrevimento de resistir, in: Carvalho Filho, S. de A. et al. (orgs.), *Deserdados: dimensões das desigualdades sociais.* Rio de Janeiro: HP Comunicação, 2007.

Cruz, M. S., Uma abordagem sobre a história da educação dos negros, in: Romão, J., *História da educação do negro e outras histórias.* Brasília: Ministério da Educação. Secretaria de Educação Continuada, Alfabetização e Diversidade, 2005.

Cunha, L. M., A população negra nos conteúdos ministrados no curso normal e nas escolas públicas primárias de Pernambuco, de 1919 a 1934, in: Romão, J., *História da educação do negro e outras histórias.* Brasília: Ministério da Educação. Secretaria de Educação Continuada, Alfabetização e Diversidade, 2005.

Cunha, O. G. da, Depois da festa: movimentos negros e políticas de identidade, in: Alvarez, S. E., Dagnino, e., Escobar, A. (orgs.), *Cultura e política nos movimentos sociais latino-americanos.* Belo Horizonte: Editora da UFMG, 2000, p. 333-82.

Damascena, A. A., O caráter formativo da congada, in: Oliveiras, I., Gonçalves, P. B., Pinto, R. P. (orgs.), *Negro e educação: escola, identidades, cultura e políticas públicas*. São Paulo: Ação Educativa, ANPEd, 2005,

p. 168-178.

Dayrell, J. T., *A música entra em cena: o rap e o* funk *na socialização da juventude*. Belo Horizonte: Editora da UFMG, 2005.

Dionisio, A. P. et al. (orgs.), *Gêneros textuais & ensino*. São Paulo: Parábola Editorial, 2010.

Erickson, F., Qualitative Methods in Research on Teaching, in: Wittrock, M. C. (orgs.), *Handbook of Research on Teaching: a Project of the American Educational Research Association*. Nova York: Macmillan Publishing Co., 1986.

___, Ethnographic Microanalysis of Interaction, in: Erickson, F., *The Handbook of Qualitative Research in Education*. Nova York: Academic Press, 1992.

Erickson, F., Shultz, J., O quando de um contexto: questões e métodos na análise de competência social, in: Ribeiro, B. T., Garcez, P. M., *Socio- linguística interacional*. São Paulo: Loyola, 2002.

Félix, J. B. J., *Chic Show e Zimbabwe a construção da identidade nos bailes* black *paulistanos*. (Mestrado). São Paulo: Faculdade de Filosofia Letras e Ciências Humanas da Universidade de São Paulo, 2000.

___, *Hip-hop: política e cultura no contexto paulistano*. (Doutorado). São Paulo: Faculdade de Filosofia, Letras e Ciências Humanas da Universidade de São Paulo, 2006.

Figueiredo, A., *Novas elites de cor: estudo sobre os profissionais liberais negros de Salvador*. São Paulo: Annablume, Sociedade Brasileira de Instrução, Centro de Estudos Afro-Asiáticos, 2002.

Fonseca, M. D., Pretos, pardos, crioulos e cabras nas escolas mineiras do século XIX, in: Romão, J., *História da educação do negro e outras histórias*. Brasília: Ministério da Educação. Secretaria de Educação Continuada, Alfabetização e Diversidade, 2005.

___, As primeiras práticas educacionais com características modernas em relação aos negros no Brasil, in: Concurso Negro e Educação, *Negro e educação: presença do negro no sistema educacional brasileiro*. São Paulo: ANPEd, Ação Educativa, 2001, p. 11-36.

Galvão, A. M. O., Oralidade, memória e a mediação do outro: práticas de letramento entre sujeitos com baixos níveis de escolarização — o caso do cordel (1930 -1950). *Educação & Sociedade*. Campinas, vol. 1, n. 1, p.

247-272.

Gatti, B. A., *Grupo focal na pesquisa em ciências sociais e humanas*. Brasília: Líber Livro Editora, 2005.

Gee, J., *Social Linguistics and Literacies. Ideologies in Discourses*. Hampshire: The Falmer Press, 1990.

Giacomini, S. M., *A alma da festa: família, etnicidade e projetos num clube social da zona norte do Rio de Janeiro: O Renascença Clube*. Belo Horizonte — Rio de Janeiro: Editora da UFMG — IUPERJ, 2006.

Giddens, A., *Sociologia*. Porto Alegre: Artmed, 2005.

Gilroy, P., *O Atlântico negro: modernidade e dupla consciência*. São Paulo — Rio de Janeiro: Ed. 34 — Universidade Candido Mendes, Centro de Estudos Afro-Asiáticos, 2001.

Gnerre, M., *Linguagem, escrita e poder*. São Paulo: Martins Fontes, 1991. Gohn, M. G., *Teoria dos movimentos sociais: paradigmas clássicos e contemporâneos*. São Paulo: Loyola, 2002.

Gomes, N. L., *Sem perder a raiz*. Belo Horizonte: Autêntica, 2006.

___, Rappers, educação e identidade racial, in: Lima, I., Romão, J., Silveira, S. M. (orgs.), *Educação popular afro-brasileira*. Florianópolis: Núcleo de Estudos Negros.

___, *A mulher negra que vi de perto: O processo de construção da identidade racial de professoras negras*. Belo Horizonte: Mazza, 1995.

___, Educação cidadã, etnia e raça: o trato pedagógico da diversidade, in: Cavalleiro, E. (org.), *Racismo e antirracismo na educação: repensando nossa escola*. São Paulo: Summus/Selo Negro, 2001.

___, Escola e diversidade étnico-cultural: um diálogo possível, in: Dayrell, J. (org.), *Múltiplos olhares sobre educação e cultura*. Belo Horizonte: Editora da UFMG, 1996.

___, Cultura negra e educação. *Revista Brasileira de Educação*, Rio de Janeiro, n. 23, 2003.

Gonçalves, L. A. O., *Silêncio: um ritual pedagógico a favor da discriminação*. (Mestrado). Belo Horizonte: Faculdade de Educação da UFMG, 1985.

___, Negro e educação no Brasil, in: *500 anos de educação no Brasil*. Belo Horizonte: Autêntica, 2000.

Gonçalves, L. A. O., Silva, P. B. G., *O jogo das diferenças: o multiculturalismo e seus contextos*. Belo Horizonte: Autêntica, 1998.

Gonçalves, M. G., *Racionais Mc's: o discurso possível de uma juventude excluída*. (Doutorado). São Paulo: Faculdade de Educação da USP, 2001.

Gonçalves, P. B., Aprender a conduzir a própria vida: dimensões do educarse entre afrodescendentes e africanos, in: Barbosa, L. M. A. et al., *De preto a afrodescendente*. São Carlos: EdUFSCar, 2003.

Guedes-Pinto, A. L. et al., Percursos de letramento de professores: narrativas em foco, in: Kleiman, A. B., Matencio, M. de L. M. (orgs.), *Letramento e formação do professor: práticas discursivas, representações e construção do saber.* Campinas: Mercado de Letras, 2005.

Guimarães, A. S. A., *Tirando a máscara: ensaios sobre o racismo no Brasil.* São Paulo: Paz e Terra, 2000.

Hall, S., *A identidade cultural na pós-modernidade.* Rio de Janeiro: DP&A, 2003a.

___, *Da diáspora: Identidade e mediações culturais.* Org.: L. Sovik; trad.: A. La Guardiã Resende ... [et al.]. Belo Horizonte — Brasília: Editora UFMG — Representação da UNESCO no Brasil, 2003b.

Hall, E. T., *A dimensão oculta.* Lisboa: Relógio D'Água Ed., 1986.

Hamilton, M., Explorando letramentos situados, in: Barton, D., Hamilton, M., Ivanic, R., (orgs.), *Situated Literacies.* Londres: Routledge, 2000, p. 1-6.

Henriques, R., *Desigualdade racial no Brasil: evolução das condições de vida na década de 90.* Rio de Janeiro: IPEA, 2001.

Herschmann, M., *O funk e o hip-hop invadem a cena.* Rio de Janeiro: Editora da UFRJ, 2000.

Hobsbawm, E., Ranger, T. (orgs.), *A invenção das tradições.* São Paulo: Paz e Terra, 2002.

Houaiss, A., Villar, M. S., Fraco, F. M. M., *Dicionário da língua portuguesa.* Rio de Janeiro: Objetiva, 2001.

Hymes, D., *Ethnography, Linguistics, Narrative Inequality: Toward a Understanding of Voice.* Bristol: Taylor & Francis, 1996.

Jovino, I. S., El *rap* como práctica cultural juvenil negra. *Boletín IFP.* Santiago, ano 2, n. 6, maio de 2004.

___, *As minas e os manos têm a palavra.* 2005. (Mestrado). São Carlos: Faculdade de Educação da UFSCAR, 2005.

Kleiman, A. B., Modelos de letramento e as práticas de alfabetização na escola, in: Kleiman, A. B. (org.), *Os significados do letramento.* Campinas: Mercado de Letras, 1995.

___, Processos identitários na formação profissional: o professor como agente de letramento, in: Correa, M., Boch, F. (orgs.), *Ensino de língua: representação e letramento.* Campinas: Mercado de Letras, 2006b.

___, Concepções da escrita na escola e formação do professor, in: Valente, A. (org.), *Aulas de português, perspectivas inovadoras.* Petrópolis: Editora Vozes, 1998.

___, *Formação do professor: processos de retextualização* e práticas de letramento. São Paulo: Fapesp, 2002.

___, *Preciso ensinar o letramento? Não basta ensinar a ler e escrever?* Campinas: Cefiel-Unicamp; MEC, 2005.

___, Leitura e prática social no desenvolvimento de competências no ensino médio, in: Bunzen, C., Mendonça, M. (orgs.), *Português no ensino médio e formação do professor*. São Paulo: Parábola Editorial, 2006a.

___, O processo de aculturação pela escrita: ensino da forma ou aprendizagem da função?, in: Kleiman, A. B., Signorini, I. (orgs.), *O ensino e a formação do professor: alfabetização de jovens e adultos*. Porto Alegre: Artmed, 2000, p. 223-243.

_, Letramento e formação do professor: quais as práticas e exigências no local de trabalho?, in: Kleiman, A. B. (org.), *A formação do professor: perspectivas da linguística aplicada*. Campinas: Mercado de Letras, 2001, p. 39-68.

___, Professores e agentes de letramento: identidade e posiciona *Revista Educação e Sociedade*, São Paulo: USP. [no prelo].

King, J., , M. E., Usando o pensamento africano e o conhecimento nativo da comunidade, in: Gomes, L. N., Silva, P. G., *Experiências etnoculturais para a formação de professores*. Belo Horizonte: Autêntica, 2002.

Koch, I. G. V., Morato, E. M., Bentes, A. C., *Referenciação e discurso*. São Paulo: Contexto, 2005.

___, *Desvendando os segredos do texto*. São Paulo: Cortez Editora, 2002. Lahire, B., *Homem plural: os determinantes da ação*. Petrópolis: Vozes, 2002.

___, *Sucesso escolar nos meios populares: as razões do improvável*. São Paulo: Ática, 1997.

Lakoff, G., Johnson, M., *Metáforas da vida cotidiana*. Campinas: Mercado de Letras, 2002.

Lima, M. N. M. de (org.), *Por que e como formar professores(as) em história e cultura afro-brasileira e africana. Escola plural*. São Paulo: Cortez, Brasília: UNICEF, Salvador: CEAFRO, 2005.

Lindolfo Filho, J., *Hip-hopper*: Tribos urbanas, metrópoles e controle social, in: Pais, J. M. E., Blass, L. M. S. (orgs.), *Tribos urbanas: produção artística e identidades*. São Paulo: Annablume, 2004.

Luz, I. M., Compassos letrados: trabalhadores negros entre a instrução e o ofício em Pernambuco (1830-1860), in: Oliveira, I., Aguiar, M. Â., Silva, P., Oliveira, R., de (orgs.), *Negro e educação 4: Linguagens, educação, resistências, políticas públicas. São Paulo: Ação Educativa, ANPED, 2008, vol. 4, p. 5-336.*

Macedo, M. J., Hora de trançar os braços, hora de dançar samba rock. *Revista Histórica do Arquivo do Estado de São Paulo e da Imprensa Oficial do Estado de São Paulo*. São Paulo, n. 15, jul-set., 2004.

Maingueneau, D., *Ethos*, cenografia, incorporação, in: Amossy, R. (org.), *Imagens de si no discurso: a construção do* ethos. São Paulo: Contexto, 2005.

Matencio, M. de L. M., *Estudo da língua falada e aula de língua materna: uma abordagem processual da interação professor/alunos*. Campinas: Mercado de Letras, 2001.

Matencio, M. de L. M., Silva, J. Q. G., Referência pessoal e jogo interlocuivo: efeitos identitários, in: Kleiman, A. B. e Matencio, M. L. M. (orgs.), *Letramento e formação do professor: práticas discursivas, representações e construção do saber*. Campinas: Mercado de Letras, 2005.

___, A leitura na formação e atuação do professor da Educação Básica, in: Mari, H. et al. (orgs.), *Ensaios sobre a leitura*. Belo Horizonte: CIPEL/ PUC-MINAS, 2005.

___, Letramento na formação do professor: integração a práticas discursivas acadêmicas e construção da identidade profissional, in: Correa, M. L. G.; Boch, F. (orgs.), *Ensino de Língua: representação e letramento*. Campinas: Mercado de Letras, 2006.

___, Referenciação e retextualização de textos acadêmicos: um estudo do resumo e da resenha, in: Congresso Internacional da ABRALIN,

III. *Anais*. Rio de Janeiro: UFRJ, 2003, p. 110- 120.

McLaren, P., Pedagogia gangsta e guetocentrismo: a nação *hip-hop* como uma esfera contrapública, in: McLaren, P., *Multiculturamismo revolucionário: pedagogia do dissenso para o novo milênio*. Porto Alegre: Artes Médicas Sul, 2000.

Magnani, J. G. C., Os circuitos dos jovens urbanos. *Tempo Social: Revista de Sociologia da USP*, São Paulo, vol. 17, n. 2, nov. 2005.

Magro, V. M. M., Adolescentes como autores de si próprios: cotidiano, educação e o *hip-hop. Caderno Cedes*, vol. 22, n. 57, ago. 2002.

Maingueneau, D., *Análise de textos de comunicação*. São Paulo: Cortez, 2004.

___, *Ethos*, cenografia, incorporação, in: Amossy, R. (org.), *Imagens de si no discurso: a construção do ethos*. São Paulo: Contexto, 2005, pp. 69-92.

Malachias, R., *Ação transcultural: a visibilidade da Juventude Negra nos bailes* black *de São Paulo (Brasil) e Havana (Cuba)*. (Mestrado). São Paulo: PROLAM, Universidade de São Paulo, 2000.

Meurer, J. L., Bonini, A., Motta-Roth, D. (orgs.). *Gêneros — teorias, métodos e debates*. São Paulo: Parábola Editorial, 2005.

Moita Lopes, L. P., *Identidades fragmentadas: a construção discursiva de raça, gênero e sexualidade em sala de aula*. Campinas: Mercado de Letras, 2002.

Morais, C. C., Ler e escrever: habilidades de escravos e forros? Comarca do Rio das Mortes, Minas Gerais, 1731-1850. *Revista Brasileira de Educação*, Rio de Janeiro, vol. 12, n. 36, set./dez. 2007.

Motta-Roth, D., Questões de metodologia em análise de gêneros, in: Karwoski, A., Gaydecza, B., Brito, K. S. (orgs.), *Gêneros textuais: reflexões e ensino*. São Paulo: Parábola Editorial, 2011.

Movimento Negro Unificado. *1978-1988: 10 anos de luta contra o racismo*. São Paulo: Confraria do Livro, 1988.

Moysés, S. M. A., Literatura e história: imagens de leitura e de leitores no Brasil no século XIX. *Revista Brasileira de Educação*, Rio de Janeiro, vol. 0, set./dez. 1995.

Munanga, K., As facetas de um racismo silenciado, in: Schwarcz, L. M., Queiroz, R. da S., *Raça e diversidade*. São Paulo: Edusp, 1996.

___, *Uma abordagem conceitual das noções de raça, racismo, identidade e etnia.* Niterói: Programa de Educação Sobre o Negro na Sociedade Brasileira, EdUFF, 2004.

Paixão, M., Carvano, L. M., *Relatório anual das desigualdades raciais no Brasil: 2007-2008.* Rio de Janeiro: Instituto de Economia da UFRJ, Editora Garamond, 2008.

Pereira, I. Ação política: fator de constituição do letramento do analfabeto adulto, in: Kleiman, A. B. (org.), *Os significados do letramento: uma nova perspectiva sobre a prática social da escrita.* Campinas: Mercado de Letras. 1995.

Pires, R. de A., *Narrativas quilombolas: Negros em contos, de Cuti e Mayombe, de Pepetela.* (Mestrado). Belo Horizonte: Universidade Federal de Minhas Gerais, 1998.

Pochmann, M., *Políticas de inclusão social.* São Paulo: Cortez, 2004. Quintão, A. A., *Irmandades negras: outro espaço de luta e resistência.* São Paulo: Annablume/ Fapesp, 2002.

Rajagopalan, K., *Por uma linguística crítica: linguagem, identidade e a questão ética.* São Paulo: Parábola Editorial, 2003.

___, Teorizando a resistência, in: Silva, D. E., Vieira, J. (org.), *Análise do discurso: percursos teóricos e metodológicos.* Brasília: UnB; Oficina Editoria do Instituto de Letras; Plano, 2002, p. 203-220.

Reid, G. A., *Negros e brancos em São Paulo (1888 — 1988).* Trad.: M. Lopes. Bauru: Edusc, 1998.

Reis, J. J., A sociedade malê: organização e proselitismo, in: Reis, J. J., *Rebelião escrava no Brasil: a história do levante dos malês em 1835.* São Paulo: Cia. das Letras, 2003.

Ribeiro, V. M., Uma perspectiva para os estudos do letramento: lições de um projeto em curso, in: Kleiman, A. B., Matencio, M. de L. M. (orgs.), *Letramento e formação do professor: práticas discursivas, representações e construção do saber.* Campinas: Mercado de Letras, 2005.

Rocha , A. M., Oficina e festival de *hip-hop* da cidade Tiradentes, in: *Jovens negros em São Paulo. Autoestima e participação.* Brasília: Fundação Cultural Palmares/ Minc. *Revista Palmares*, n. 4, p. 11, out. 2000.

Rojo, R., *Letramentos múltiplos, escola e inclusão social.* São Paulo: Parábola Editorial, 2009.

Sader, E., *Quando novos personagens entraram em cena. Experiências, falas e lutas dos trabalhadores da Grande São Paulo (1970-1980)*. Rio de Janeiro: Paz e Terra, 1988.

Santos, H., *A busca de um caminho para o Brasil. A trilha do círculo vicioso*. São Paulo: Editora SENAC São Paulo, 2001.

Santos, M., Território e dinheiro, in: Programa de Pós-Graduação em Geografia da UFF. *Território, Territórios*. Niterói: PPGEO-UFF/AGB, 2002.

Shusterman, R., *Vivendo a arte: o pensamento pragmatista e a estética popular*. São Paulo: Editora 34, 1998.

Silva, A. M. P., *Aprender com perfeição e sem coação: uma escola para meninos pretos e pardos na Corte*. Brasília: Editora Plano, 2002.

Silva, J. C. G., Arte e educação: a experiência do movimento *hip-hop* paulistano, in: Silva, J. C. G., *Rap e educação. Rap é educação*. São Paulo: Selo Negro (Summus), 1999.

Silva, T. T. (org.), *Identidade e diferença: a perspectiva dos estudos culturais*. Petrópolis: Vozes, 2000.

Silva, V. G. da, *O antropólogo e sua magia: trabalho de campo e texto etnográfico nas pesquisas antropológicas sobre religiões afro-brasileiras*. São Paulo: EDUSP, 2000.

Silva, J. C. G., *Rap na cidade de São Paulo: música, etnicidade e experiência urbana. 1998*. (Doutorado). Campinas: UNICAMP, 1998.

___, A arte e educação: a experiência do movimento *hip-hop* paulistano, in: Andrade, E., *Rap e educação: rap é educação*. São Paulo: Sumus/Selo Negro, 1999.

Silva, P. B. G., Aprender a conduzir a própria vida: dimensões do educar-se entre afrodescendentes e africanos, in: Silva, P. B. G. et al. (orgs.), *De preto a afrodescendente: trajetos de pesquisa sobre relações* étnico-*raciais no Brasil*. São Carlos: Edufscar, 2003, p. 181-97.

___, Dimensões e sobrevivências de pensamentos em educação em territórios africanos e afro-brasileiros, in: Lima, I., Silveira, S. M. (orgs.), *Negros, territórios e educação*. Florianópolis: Núcleo de Estudos Negros, n. 7 (nov/2000), p. 378-388.

Sodré, M., *A verdade seduzida*. Rio de Janeiro: Francisco Alves, 1988. Souza, A. L. S. et al., *De Olho na cultura: um ponto de vista afro-brasileiro*. Salvador — Brasília: Centro de Estudos Afro-Orientais (CEAO/ UFBA) — Fundação Cultural Palmares, 2005.

Stam, R., *Bakhtin: da teoria literária* à *cultura de massa*. São Paulo: Ática, 1992.

Street, B. V., *Literacy in Theory and Practice*. Cambridge: Cambridge University Press, 1984.

Tápias-Oliveira, E. M., *Construção identitária profissional no ensino superior: prática diarista e formação do professor.* (Doutorado). Campinas: Programa de Pós-Graduação em Linguística Aplicada, Unicamp, 2006.

Theodoro, M. (org.), *As políticas públicas e a desigualdade racial no Brasil: 120 anos após a abolição.* Brasília: IPEA, 2008.

Vieira, L., *Cidadania e globalização.* Rio de Janeiro: Record, 1998.

Vovio, C. L., Souza, A. L. S., Desafios metodológicos em pesquisas sobre letramento, in: Kleiman, A. B., Matencio, M. de L. M. (orgs.), *Letramento e formação do professor: práticas discursivas, representações e construção do saber.* Campinas: Mercado de Letras, 2005.

Vovio, C. L., *Entre discursos: sentidos, práticas e identidades leitoras de alfabetizadores de jovens e adultos.* (Doutorado). Campinas: IEL/UNI- CAMP, 2007.

TRANSCRIPT CONVENTIONS

Transcription conventions based on Cristiane M Schnack, Thaís D. Pisoni & Ana Cristina Ostermann. 2005. *Transcrição de fala: do evento real* à representação escrita. (São Leopoldo: Entrelinhas, 2005).	
= Connected speech	Indicates that there is no space between a speaker's speech and the speech XX: when I knew [text] XX
(1.2) Pause	Pause is measured in seconds or tenths of seconds. Represents the absence of speech or vocalization.
(.) Micropause	Equivalent to less than 0.2 seconds of no speech or vocalization.
, Continuous intonation	Indicates continuous intonation, as when listing items
. Falling intonation	Indicates falling intonation
? Rising intonation	Indicates rising intonation
- Abrupt interruption of speech	Abrupt interruption of an ongoing speech
: Sound stretching	Indicates vowel or consonant prolongation
>text< Fast-paced speech	Indicates faster speech relative to the previous and post situations of the speech

<text> Slow-paced speech	Indicates slower speech
°text° Speak in a lower volume	Indicates speech in a low volume
TEXT Louder tone	Indicates speech at a loud volume
Text Stressed syllable, word or sound	Indicates stressed syllable, word or sound
↑↓ Arrows	Indicates an increase or decrease in intonation
hhh	Audible expiration
.hhh	Indicates that the following sound is spoken on in-breath
(text) Doubts	Indicates speech that cannot be deciphered, or where the transcription is dubious
XXXX inaudible	Indicates syllables that were not possible to transcribe
((text)) Comment s	Transcriber's Comments
@@@ Laughter	Indicates laughter

ABOUT THE AUTHORS AND CONTRIBUTORS

AUTHOR

DRA. ANA LÚCIA SILVA SOUZA

I am a child of Brazil's Black Social Movements. I am an activist, an educator, a reader of the world. I have a degree in political and social sciences, a master's degree in social sciences, a doctorate and a postdoctoral degree in applied linguistics. I am a professor at the Federal University of Bahia, at the Institute of Letters. I lead the research group RASURAS: Literacies of Reexistence in the Black Diaspora. I am affiliated to the Brazilian Association of Black Researchers - ABPN. I am a part of the board of directors of the NGO Ação Educativa. In my research I've been diving into uses of language, literacy, hip-hop culture, youth and affirmative action. I have several publications, including the book Literacies of Reexistence – Poetry, Graffiti, Music, Dance - Hip-Hop and also Literacies in High School Ed. Parable.

TRANSLATORS

FEVA OMO IYANU

Feva Omo Iyanu (M.A. Federal University of Bahia, Portuguese and English) is a translator, writer and professor of Afro-Brazilian and African Literature, developing his research in the field of Translation Studies, Ethnic and Aphrodiasporic Studies, Afro-Brazilian Religiosity and Literature of black Afrodiasporic and African writings. Author of Sobre a Pretintura dos Olhos Negros, Feva is a scholar of Yoruba Cultures and their influence on the Brazilian diaspora. His literary productions and translational methodological processes are based on the principles of the Black-African ethics of being, living and experiencing the world.

TANYA L. SAUNDERS

Dr. Tanya L. Saunders is a sociologist interested in the ways in which the African Diaspora throughout the Americas uses the arts as a tool for social change. As a 2011-2012 Fulbright scholar in Brazil, Dr. Saunders began work on their current project about Black Queer Artivism in Brazil. Dr. Saunders is the founder and editor-in-chief of Améfrica Press. Their book on Cuban Underground Hip-Hop has been published in Portuguese.

AYALA TUDE

Ayala Tude is an English teacher, translator and holds a Master's in Literature and Culture from the Federal University of Bahia (UFBA). Additionally, Ayala served as an Associate Researcher at the group "Translating in the Black Atlantic," where her work delved into the realms of translation, literature and cultural identities. She is also a co-founder of Afro Di-aspora Connect, an English course that embraces a non- traditional approach, with the goal of fostering language acquisition within the context of African Diasporic cultures and histories.

COVER ART

ANTHONY SMITH JR.

I make artwork that's filled with rich dense spaces. These spaces coalesce into vibrant and sometimes floral worlds where I often play out moral, political or philosophical fantasies using calligraphic gestures and collage. I often layer and erase work to cap-ture the ghost of what came before. I see the mission of my art as attempting to describe the world without the filters we have creat-ed to make sense of that world. The visual onslaughts I create make passing attempts at establishing balance in the traditional sense but more often than not represent a form of visual static rather than compositional harmony. www.anthonysmithjr.com

www.ingramcontent.com/pod-product-compliance
Lightning Source LLC
Chambersburg PA
CBHW070112030426
42335CB00016B/2119